D1218442

Discussions of the Divine Comedy

DISCUSSIONS OF LITERATURE

General Editor JOSEPH H. SUMMERS, Washington University

Edited by

WORKS

The Canterbury Tales	CHARLES A. OWEN, JR., University of Connecticut
The Divine Comedy	IRMA BRANDEIS, Bard College
Hamlet	J. C. LEVENSON, University of Minnesota
Moby-Dick	MILTON R. STERN, University of Connecticut
Shakespeare's Histories	R. J. DORIUS, University of Hamburg
Shakespeare's Problem Comedies	ROBERT ORNSTEIN, University of Illinois
Shakespeare's Roman Plays	MAURICE CHARNEY, Rutgers University
Shakespeare's Sonnets	BARBARA HERRNSTEIN, Bennington College

AUTHORS

Jane Austen	WILLIAM HEATH, Amherst College
William Blake	JOHN E. GRANT, University of Connecticut
Charles Dickens	WILLIAM ROSS CLARK, University of Connecticut
John Donne	FRANK KERMODE, University of Manchester
George Eliot	RICHARD STANG, Washington University, St. Louis
Henrik Ibsen	JAMES WALTER MCFARLANE, King's College, University of Durham
Henry James	NAOMI LEBOWITZ, Washington University, St. Louis
Alexander Pope	RUFUS A. BLANSHARD, University of Connecticut
Jonathan Swift	JOHN TRAUGOTT, University of California, Berkeley
Mark Twain	GUY A. CARDWELL, Washington University, St. Louis
William Wordsworth	JACK M. DAVIS, University of Connecticut

GENRES

Modern American Drama	WALTER MESERVE, University of Kansas
Poetry: Form and Structure	FRANCIS MURPHY, Smith College
Poetry: Rhythm and Sound	GEORGE HEMPHILL, University of Connecticut
The Novel	ROGER SALE, University of Washington
The Short Story	HOLLIS SUMMERS, Ohio University

DISCUSSIONS

OF

THE DIVINE COMEDY.

Edited with an Introduction by

Irma Brandeis

BARD COLLEGE

D. C. Heath and Company

BOSTON

CONTENTS

I. Before the Twentieth Century

GIOVANNI BOCCACCIO, *from* The First Lecture to the Florentine
    Commune   1
PETRARCH, Letter to Boccaccio   6
GIAMBATTISTA VICO, Discovery of the True Dante   11
VOLTAIRE, Dante   13
SAMUEL TAYLOR COLERIDGE, Dante   16
UGO FOSCOLO, A Parallel between Dante and Petrarch   21
GOETHE, A Discussion of Dante   32
JOHN RUSKIN, Dante's Landscape   33
GIOSUÈ CARDUCCI, Lecture on Dante   42

II. The Twentieth Century

MICHELE BARBI, Genesis and Composition of the *Divine Comedy*   46
BENEDETTO CROCE, Aesthetic Criteria   49
LUIGI MALAGOLI, The Substantive Penchant   52
ERICH AUERBACH, Figural Art in the *Divine Comedy*   56
PHILIP H. WICKSTEED, Hell   63
FRANCIS FERGUSSON, The Metaphor of the Journey   69
CHARLES S. SINGLETON, The Pattern at the Center   75
ETIENNE GILSON, The Transfiguration of Beatrice   84
JEFFERSON B. FLETCHER, The "Three Blessed Ladies" of the
    Divine Comedy   91
ALLEN TATE, The Symbolic Imagination: A Meditation on
    Dante's Three Mirrors   102
T. S. ELIOT, A Talk on Dante   112

INTRODUCTION

HARDLY MORE than fifty years after Dante's death in 1321 the "discussions," public and notable, of his great poem began; and the stream of criticism that then sprang up, although it has in certain periods run very thin, or merely babbled, in our own times has become a torrent. Such, indeed, are the numbers and the energy of its tributaries that one is sometimes led to think the last needed or wanted word on the subject must already have been spoken. But of course that is not—and, in the final analysis, happily is not—so. Every age reads Dante with its own capacities, and raises its own fresh questions. Every new period receives the fruit of the earlier studies and may, if it chooses, move forward with an advantage. And the poem itself, the *Divine Comedy*, available though it is in many ways to every reader who cares to venture into it, proves ultimately such a network of interlocking images, meanings, and forms as never to be fully and finally available to any reader.

The discussions that have reached us began in Florence when the Commune invited Giovanni Boccaccio, in his old age, to deliver a series of public readings and comments on the book of the poet who had died in exile. That century, the fourteenth, produced no fewer than six illustrious commentaries on the *Comedy*—not works of criticism in the modern sense, but mines of invaluable information and suggestion on the historical, political, linguistic materials of the poem. For a while Dante's reputation flourished throughout Europe. Then in the fifteenth and sixteenth centuries it fell away. The new writers found the poet unpolished, blunt, formless—in a word, "barbarous." And this notion persisted. Giambattista

Vico, in the eighteenth century, was one of the first to deride the "effeminacy" of taste that had produced such a view, and to call for a new sort of reading of the old book. And as the Age of Reason waned, estimation of Dante rose again. When the Romantic movement sought to break with the retrospective philosophic and aesthetic norms of a "classical" age, what had been Dante's sins—his individual passion, his mixing of the poetic genres, his mysticism—became his virtues; and he drew again great numbers of readers and critics. The secret depths of the poem began to emerge to view, and at the same time the field for scholarly exegesis began to attract more serious students. Today it is impossible to describe Dante's reputation and influence: every conceivable evaluation of him has its followers, and every camp, from the sentimental to the new-critical, its printed spokesmen. Thus a Dante bibliography for the years 1940–49 [1] was able to list a total of 1152 published items, of which 307 were concerned exclusively with the *Divine Comedy*, while hundreds of others involved it in various kinds of comparative studies. One has no reason to expect the listing for the following decade to be smaller.

In the face of such floods of Dante discussions, the reader may well inquire what principles of selection have been used to shape the present anthology. I shall try to answer. Assuming that all the odds were against arriving at any true representation of the full range of Dante criticism, I have granted myself a free hand in assembling what I thought most valuable for present-

[1] Aldo Vallone, *Gli Studi Danteschi dal 1940 al 1949*, Florence, Olschki, 1950.

day students. My effort has been to put before the reader a sampling of good (though occasionally merely piquant) talk about the *Divine Comedy* from Dante's age to our own. I have passed over entirely the vast body of scholarly research and historical commentary of which the serious student must eventually make use, have regretfully excluded selections of great length that could not reasonably be clipped to 6000 words or fewer, and have omitted certain celebrated essays currently available in most libraries and bookstores. Further, in order to offer the largest possible number and variety of discussions, I have taken the liberty of cutting, where it seemed possible to do so without injuring the writer's drift.

The resulting book is divided into two parts. Part I consists of essays in historical sequence, beginning in Dante's own times and ending in the latter years of the nineteenth century. Here it has seemed sensible to limit the selection to critics who are themselves writers of international fame, and even to admit two or three of these on the basis of trivial or impudent remarks, because of the intrinsic interest, for the student, of the source. Greatest emphasis is on the nineteenth century, when the interest in Dante became more serious and widespread in Europe and the United States, and when the *Comedy* began to be discussed as a living poem rather than as a monument or an icon. But the reader must be warned that many important names are missing: among others, those of Hegel, the two Schlegels, Shelley, Carlyle—not to speak of the specializing scholars such as Karl Witte in Germany and Edward Moore in England.

Part II is made up of twentieth-century discussions. Here the order rests on a rough division of subject matter. The first two essays are introductory: one, to the circumstances surrounding the writing of the *Comedy*; the other, very briefly, to the problem of aesthetic judgment. There follow a study of language and one of allegorical method. In the next six selections attention is fo-

cused on particular portions of the *Comedy* in close and serious study of texture and intent; although the approaches differ, there is a certain harmony among them, and each, it is hoped, will be suggestive to the student in his own further study. In the final selection a living poet speaks of the influence of the old one upon his own work.

Discussions 3–10 in this second part have been chosen on the basis of their capacity, as they stand, to illuminate depths and subtleties of the poem which are apt to elude first—even second and subsequent—readings. For Dante's great work is elusive—and curiously so. As I have already remarked, it is in one sense simple and immediately available: the first countenance it offers us is that of a dramatic and straightforward narrative describing a journey through hell, purgatory, and paradise, weighted by certain lessons and excursions into philosophy and theology which we may, if we wish, pass over hastily. If we choose to stop with a simple literal reading, we will still know something of what Dante intended and may still have heard correctly many of the beauties of the poem. But beneath, or beyond, this first countenance of the *Comedy* lies an infinitely complex articulation of its detail, which alters and develops what one sees, and broadens, deepens, and relates its meanings to such an extent that the reader who knows the poem best is the first to admit the unlikeliness of ever completing, much less exhausting, its experience.

The new methods of twentieth-century criticism must be thanked for bringing much of this second countenance to light. Writers of the earlier periods, seeking to elucidate the poem by historical research and by an interpretation that assumed the "allegory" to have no complexities which an adequate knowledge of theology and history would not solve, missed the finer relations of part to part and failed to see or feel the larger work of the symbolic imagination. The nineteenth century made great advances both in scholarly and stylistic studies, but it separated the two, and tended to distribute its interest piecemeal upon intellectual matters, lyric beauties, history, language, and the like. It remained for the twentieth-century critics to bring together scholarship, poetic interest, and the methods of close textual study. And so we have today scholarly studies that elucidate the poem, comments on the poetics of the *Comedy* informed by knowledge of Dante's times and traditions, and textual analysis which, by bringing the reader's eye to bear closely on what is there before him, teaches him to find for himself the secret footholds of the towering poem.

The student in search of further readings will find Umberto Cosmo's *A Handbook to Dante Studies* (Oxford, 1950) a helpful guide to Dante criticism from the fourteenth century to approximately 1945, primarily in the European languages. He should see in addition Angelina La Piana's *Dante's American Pilgrimage* (New York, 1948). Useful selected Dante bibliographies will also be found in three much recommended works: H. F. Dunbar's *Symbolism in Medieval Thought and Its Consummation in the Divine Comedy* (New Haven, 1929); Bernard Stambler's *Dante's Other World* (New York, 1957); Karl Vossler's *Medieval Culture—An Introduction to Dante and His Times* (London, 1929). The Dante Society of America issues in its annual report a bibliography with brief résumés of new books, articles, editions, etc.

Of contemporary discussions omitted from this anthology for reasons specified above, the editor would like especially to mention here George Santayana's Dante chapter in *Three Philosophical Poets,* T. S. Eliot's longer essay, entitled "Dante," and Jacques Maritain's "Dante's Innocence—and Luck" in his *Creative Intuition in Art and Poetry.*

IRMA BRANDEIS

The *Divine Comedy*

Giovanni Boccaccio

from The First Lecture to the Florentine Commune

"All men who have any degree of right feeling, at the beginning of every enterprise, whether small or great, call upon God. And we, too, . . . if we be not altogether out of our wits, must invoke divine aid and pray that our words may be acceptable. . . ."[1] And if Plato thus confesses himself greatly in need of divine aid, what ought I to presume, aware as I am of the slowness of my mind, my small ability, and my fleeting memory? Knowing further that I am about to take upon myself a weight greater than my shoulders can bear —namely, to explain the artful text, the many narratives, the sublime meanings hidden under the poetic veil of the *Comedy* of our Dante; and, above all, that I am to do this in the presence of men of such lofty understanding and deep perspicacity as you are universally known to be, Signori of Florence—surely my need must be great beyond that of any other man. Wherefore, in order that what I am about to say may be honor and glory to the name of God, and aid and consolation to my hearers, I desire before proceeding further to invoke as humbly as I may the help of God— and with far more confidence in his benignity than in any merit of mine. And since what we are about to speak of is poetry, let me now make poetic invocation of such aid in the words of the Trojan Anchises as Virgil sets them down in the second book of the *Aeneid*:

Iupiter omnipotens, precibus si flecteris ullis,
aspice nos: hoc tantum: et, si pietate meremur,
da deinde auxilium, pater. . . .[2]

Now, having besought the divine clemency to lend its grace to the present task, I deem that three things which generally precede any such study as this, must be undertaken before we approach the letter of the text: namely, an enumeration and description of the causes of the work; a consideration of its title; and an indication of the branch of philosophy to which it belongs.

The causes of this book are four:

[1] For Boccaccio's Latin version the editor has substituted Jowett's English: from the *Timaeus*, 27.

[2] Jupiter omnipotent, if thou art moved by any prayers, look upon us at this moment; and if we merit pity, give then thy aid, Father. . . .

From the first lecture of the first public reading and commentary on the *Divine Comedy*, begun in the year 1373 in the church of Santo Stefano di Badia, at the request of the Florentine Commune. Translated by the present editor from the Italian as given in G. Boccaccio, *Il Comento alla Divina Commedia e gli altri scritti intorno a Dante*, edited by Domenico Guerra, Bari, Laterza, 1918. Notes by the present editor.

material, formal, efficient, and final. The material cause, like the subject of the work (which is one with its matter), is twofold; for the subject according to the literal sense is one thing and according to the allegorical sense, another; and both senses are to be found in the present book, as will manifestly appear as we go on. The subject according to the literal sense is, then, the state of souls after the death of the body, simply; since from this and concerning it the whole progress of the present work develops. The subject according to the allegorical sense is: the way in which man in the freedom of his will becomes, by merit or failure, subject to rewarding or punishing justice.

The formal cause is similarly twofold, since we have both the form of the treatise and the form of the treatment. The form of the treatise is divided into three according to the triple division of the book. The first of these divisions is that whereby the whole work is divided—namely into three canticles; the second is that whereby each canticle is broken up into cantos; the third comprises the division of each canticle into lines. The form, or mode, of treatment is poetic, fictive, descriptive, digressive, and transumptive; it is furthermore made up of definition, division, proof, refutation, and the setting forth of examples.[3] The efficient cause of the work is that same author, Dante Alighieri, of whom we shall speak more at length when we discuss the title of his poem. The final cause of the work is to remove those living in this world from a state of misery and lead them to the state of felicity.

The second of our three chief tasks is to establish the title of the work we are considering, which some say is the following: "Here begins the Comedy of Dante Alighieri, Florentine"; while others, more closely following the author's intention, say the title is: "Here begin the canticles of the Comedy of the Florentine Dante Ali-

[3] Here and elsewhere compare Dante's letter to Can Grande, which Boccaccio appears to know.

ghieri." These latter derive their claim from the title of the first division of the poem, namely: "Here begins the first canticle of the canticles of the Comedy of Dante Alighieri." But since we can here advance no proof, we shall leave the matter to the judgment of these other writers, and turn to the question of why the author felt he should so entitle his book; and we refer to the second of these titles, since the cause of the first (and most generally accepted) will be contained within the second. Let us take note that, just as musicians form all their compositions upon certain long and short, bright and grave time-measurements together with their variations, all bound with due and measured proportion, and call the resultant works "songs" (canti), so also poets—and not only those who compose in Latin, but also those, like our present author, who use the vulgar tongue—obedient to the quality of their differing medium, compose their verses of a given number of lines rhyming with mutual consonance at fixed intervals. Thus in the present work we see that every line has the same number of syllables, and that the third line of each group rhymes with the first. Wherefore it seems that the same name that composers of music give to their inventions—namely, as we have already said, "*canti*"—is suitable for such works composed in verse; and consequently a work composed of many cantos must be called a canticle—in other words, a composition containing in itself many cantos.

We observe next that in the title of this work it is called a comedy. Now we know that poetic narrative may be executed in a variety of different modes—as, for example, tragedy, satire and comedy, bucolics, elegy, lyric, and so on. But, touching the one of these which enters into the present title, some men would have it that "comedy" poorly suits this book; and they base their argument first on the meaning of the word itself, and then on the style of the comic writers, which, it seems, is quite different from that of the author of this book. They say that the matter of the book is unsuitable to the sense of the word, since comedy means rural song— being derived from the Latin *comos,* meaning farm, and *odos,* meaning song; and the rural songs, as we know, are made of humble stuff, treating of crops and cattle, or of rough and base loves and country customs; and there is no conformity at all between these things and the things narrated in any part of the present work. For the present work treats of lofty persons, of singular and notable deeds performed by virtuous and wicked men, of the effects of penitence, of the habits of angels, and of the divine essence. Furthermore, the comic style is humble and subdued, conforming to its matter—and here again it differs from the present work. For, although it be written in the vulgar tongue—in which, they say, young ladies chatter—it is nonetheless elegant, delicate, and sublime; nor do such qualities appear in the vulgar of females chattering. I do not say, however, that it would not be more artful and sublime were it written in Latin verse (without loss of those values that are in the vulgar wording), for there is more art and gravity in Latin than in the maternal language.

Concerning the method proper to the writer of comedy: he must refrain from intruding himself as a speaker, but must instead contrive that others, whom he may bring into conversation together in various times and places and for various reasons, shall set forth and develop the theme of his comedy. The author of the present book, on the contrary, very often throughout the whole work speaks his own mind both concerning himself and concerning others. Again, it is not the usage of comedy to include stories or comparisons except such as inhere in the proposed theme; whereas in this poem there are infinite numbers of comparisons and stories that have no bearing on the principal line of intent. Furthermore, comedy tells of things which, although not so remote from human behaviour in their nature as to be impossible, yet have not actually come to pass; while the substantial story of the present book—of the condemnation of those who die in sin to perpetual pain, and of the elevation of those who die in God's grace to eternal glory—is true and forever holy according to the Catholic faith. Writers of comedy, moreover, call the parts into which their works are divided "scenes." This they do because the recitation of the comedy takes place in that central part of the theater which is called the "scene," and is the place where the mimes make their appearance before the spectators, in order, as the persons they are to represent are called up. But our author calls the parts of his *Comedy* "cantos." And thus, in order to bring our discussion to an end, it seems true, as has been said, that the name "comedy" does not suit this work. Nor can one say that this name was not intended by the author—as has sometimes been the case with respect to one work or another of some author—for he, himself, calls it so in the twenty-first canto of the first canticle, saying: "Thus we moved from bridge to bridge, speaking of other matters which my Comedy has no reason to set down." What then are we to say to the objections here advanced? I should say as follows: that this writer, being an extremely sagacious man, chose his title with regard, not to the parts of comedy but to the whole, and that he named his book for the whole, figuratively. And comedy as a whole (judging as well as we can by the examples of Plautus and Terence, who were comic poets) lies in this: a turbulent beginning, full of noise and discord, and a termination in peace and tranquillity. Of which definition the present book is perfectly exemplary, since it begins with the commotions and sufferings of hell, and ends in the repose and peace of such glory as the blest possess eternally. And this ought to suffice to show that the name given is appropriate within reason to the book of which we speak.

The task that remains is to say who the writer of this book was—as indeed we ought to do in the case of every book, in order that credence not be foolishly given where it is not merited. . . .

The author of this work, as its title testifies, was Dante Alighieri, by ancestry a nobleman of our city. His life was not smooth in its course, but plagued with many changes and frequent shifts to new branches of study, so that we cannot properly speak of it without considering these studies. First, during his boyhood in his native city he devoted himself to the liberal arts, and in them made marvelous progress; for, in addition to his accomplishments in his first art, he was, as we shall show, a fine logician, a master of rhetoric (as clearly appears in his writings), and, since the work before us indicates a knowledge of astronomy, and this cannot be attained without geometry and arithmetic, I judge that he was similarly educated in both latter arts. In a similar way one is led to conclude that he must during his youth have studied, and wonderfully well imbibed, moral philosophy—for he shows no desire to conceal it in the eleventh canto of the *Inferno* where he has Virgil say: "Have you forgotten those words in which your Ethics says . . ." etc., as though he wished it to be understood that he was particularly and notably familiar with moral philosophy. In the same fashion one is led to deduce that he heard the poets and studied the historians; and furthermore one gathers from his talk with Brunetto Latini, who was reputed a man of great learning in natural philosophy, that Dante must have had an excellent foundation in that branch. But, strong though his bent may have been for these studies, he was also urgently moved by the passion we are wont to call "love," and equally by his solicitude for public honors, which he sought after ardently up to the time when, matters having gone against him and the followers of his faction, his own peril compelled him to leave Florence. After his departure he traveled about Italy for several years, thinking he would find some way of return to his own city; and when that hope was lost he betook himself to Paris and there dedicated himself to hearing teachers in natural philosophy and theology. In these studies he made such progress in a short time that he won great praise from worthy men for certain of his scholastic performances, such as public speaking, reading, and disputation. After this, he returned to Italy, and in his fifty-sixth year his trials and his life came to an end at Ravenna. He died a Catholic Christian and was honorably buried near the church of the Minor Friars. Neither the titles nor the honors proper to the teacher were ever bestowed on him, nor the laurel he had hoped—as he himself testifies in the twenty-fifth canto of the *Paradiso*—to receive in his native city. Rather did death forestall all he had desired, as we have told. His manners were grave and weighty, and almost altogether praiseworthy; but since I have already written of these things in a little book in his praise,[4] I do not care to enlarge further upon them here. But such are these matters that whoever examines them with unwarped mind must surely esteem this writer worthy of his credence and honor in whatsoever matter he sets forth in his *Comedy*.

But there remains yet something to say of his name—and first of all with regard to its meaning, which fairly well speaks for itself: for any person who gives away with liberal spirit those things he has received in grace from God, may fitly be called *Dante*.[5] And that this man gave willingly, the effect does not conceal. Before all who may wish to partake he has set out this singular and dear treasure wherein honorable delight and redemptive aid in equal shares are to be found by any man who seeks them with energy and ardor of mind. And since this gift seemed to him

[4] Boccaccio refers to his own *Trattatello in Laude di Dante*.
[5] *Dante* means *"giving."*

most excellent, both for the reasons I have just named and because it had been wrought only with much travail, long nights of work and continuous study, he was not satisfied to have the name Dante by the mere casual choice of his parents; wherefore, in order to show that it had been given him by the will of heaven, he caused himself to be called Dante by two exalted persons in his book. The first of these is Beatrice, when she has made her appearance before him on the triumphal chariot of the celestial host on the summit of Purgatory. Here she represents sacred theology, and must therefore be understood to comprehend every divine mystery, and this among others: that it is according to divine disposition that he is called Dante. In confirmation of which she herself so names him in that part of the thirtieth canto where she says: "Dante, perchè Virgilio se ne vada . . ." [6] leaving us to conclude that if she had not known him worthy, either she would not have named him at all, or would have called him otherwise. Furthermore, his naming at this point makes clear that he has arrived at a stage where, being *Dante,* he can hope to have access without Virgil (that is, without poetry—or, we might say, without worldly reason) to divine things. The other person who calls him by his name is Adam, our first father, to whom God permitted that he

give all created things their names; and, since it is thought that he named them well, the poet, by putting his own name on Adam's lips, signifies that it had been suitably bestowed. This he does in the twenty-sixth canto of the *Paradiso,* where Adam says: "Dante, la voglia tua discerno meglio. . . ." [7] And let this suffice with respect to the title of the work.

The third of the chief things I proposed to examine was the question of the branch of philosophy to which the present work belongs. According to my judgment it must be classed with the moral branch, namely ethics; for, however speculative the approach in any given passage, it is not entered upon for speculation's sake, but for the sake of the work itself.

Now, having completed the three preliminary tasks, I shall turn to the rubric: "Here begins the first canto of the *Inferno.*" But before I do so, bearing in mind the multitude of materials which will confront me in this reading, the slightness of my capacity, and the weakness of my memory, I ask that if from lack of insight or from ignorance I should utter anything infringing upon Catholic truth, it be held as unsaid; and herewith I revoke it and submit myself therein to the emendation of the Holy Church. . . .

[6] Purg. XXX, 55: "Dante, because Virgil leaves you. . . ."

[7] "Dante, I better see your wish. . . ." Unfortunately Boccaccio's reading of Par. XXVI, 104 is not the generally accepted one, and Adam no longer calls the poet by his name.

Petrarch

Letter to Boccaccio

THERE are many, things in your letter which do not require any answer; those, for example, which we have lately settled face to face. Two points there were, however, which it seemed to me should not be passed over in silence, and I will briefly write down such reflections concerning them as may occur to me. In the first place, you excuse yourself with some heat for seeming to praise unduly a certain poet, a fellow-citizen of ours, who in point of style is very popular, and who has certainly chosen a noble theme. You beg my pardon for this, as if I regarded anything said in his, or anyone else's praise, as detracting from my own. You assert, for instance, that if I will only look closely at what you say of him, I shall find that it all reflects glory upon me. You take pains to explain, in extenuation of your favourable attitude towards him, that he was your first light and guide in your early studies. Your praise is certainly only a just and dutiful acknowledgment of his services, an expression of what I may call filial piety. If we owe all to those who begot and brought us forth, and much to those who are the authors of our fortunes, what shall we say of our debt to the parents and fashioners of our minds? How much more, indeed, is due to those who refine the mind than to those who tend the body, he will perceive who assigns to each its just value; for the one, it will be seen, is an immortal gift, the other, corruptible and destined to pass away.

Continue, then, not by my sufferance simply, but with my approbation, to extol and cherish this poet, the guiding star of your intellect, who has afforded you courage and light in the arduous way by which you are pressing stoutly on towards a most glorious goal. He has long been buffeted and wearied by the windy plaudits of the multitude. Honour him now and exalt him by sincere praise worthy alike of you and of him, and, you may be sure, not unpleasing to me. He is worthy of such a herald, while you, as you say, are the natural one to assume the office. I therefore accept your song of praise with all my heart, and join with you in extolling the poet you celebrate therein.[1]

Hence there was nothing in your letter of explanation to disturb me except the discovery that I am still so ill understood by you who, as I firmly believed, knew me thoroughly. You think, then, that I do not take pleasure in the praises of illustrious men and glory in them? Believe me, nothing is more foreign to me than jealousy; there is no scourge of which I know less. On the contrary, in order that you may see how far I am from such feelings, I call upon Him before whom all hearts are open to witness that few things in life have caused me more pain than to see the meritorious passed by, utterly without

[1] This refers to the poem . . . with which Boccaccio accompanied his copy of Dante. [This and the footnotes that follow throughout the letter are from the Robinson and Rolfe volume.]

Reprinted (as translated from the original Latin) from *Petrarch, the First Modern Scholar and Man of Letters*, edited and translated by James Harvey Robinson with the collaboration of H. W. Rolfe, New York and London, G. P. Putnam, 1898. Francesco Petrarca is thought to have written this letter (here printed with omissions) in 1359.

recognition or reward. Not that I am deploring my own lot, or looking for personal gain; I am mourning the common fate of mankind, as I behold the reward of the nobler arts falling to the meaner. I am not unaware that although the reputation which attaches to right conduct may stimulate the mind to deserve it, true virtue is, as the philosophers say, a stimulus to itself; it is its own reward, its own guide, its own end and aim. Nevertheless, now that you have yourself suggested a theme which I should not voluntarily have chosen, I shall proceed to refute for you, and through you for others, the commonly accepted notion of my judgment of this poet. It is not only false, as Quintilian says of the construction put upon his criticism of Seneca,[2] but it is insidious and, with many, out-and-out malevolent. My enemies say that I hate and despise him, and in this way stir up the common herd against me, for with them he is extremely popular. This is indeed a novel kind of perversity, and shows a marvellous aptitude for harming others. But truth herself shall defend me.

In the first place, there can be no possible cause for ill-will towards a man whom I never saw but once, and that in my very earliest childhood. He lived with my grandfather and my father,[3] being younger than the former, but older than my father, with whom, on the same day and by the same

civil commotion, he was driven from his country into exile. At such a time strong friendships are often formed between companions in misery. This proved especially true of these two men, since in their case not only a similar fate but a community of taste and a love for the same studies, served to bring them together. My father, however, forced by other cares and by regard for his family, succumbed to the natural influences of exile, while his friend resisted, throwing himself, indeed, with even greater ardour into what he had undertaken, neglecting everything else and desirous alone of future fame. In this I can scarce admire and praise him enough,—that neither the injustice of his fellow-citizens, nor exile, nor poverty, nor the attacks of his enemies, neither the love of wife, nor solicitude for his children, could divert him from the path he had once decided upon, when so many who are highly endowed are yet so weak of purpose that they are swerved from their course by the least disturbance. And this most often happens to writers of verse, for silence and quiet are especially requisite for those who have to care not only for the thought and the words but the felicitous turn as well. Thus you will see that my supposed hate for this poet, which has been trumped up by I know not whom, is an odious and ridiculous invention, since there is absolutely no reason for such repugnance, but, on the contrary, every reason for partiality, on account of our common country, his friendship with my father, his genius, and his style, the best of its kind, which must always raise him far above contempt.

This brings us to the second reproach cast upon me, which is based upon the fact that, although in my early years I was very eager in my search for books of all kinds, I never possessed a copy of this poet's work, which would naturally have attracted me most at that age. While exceedingly anxious to obtain other books which I had little hope of finding, I showed a strange indifference, quite foreign

[2] Quintilian's strictures on Seneca's style had given rise to the opinion that he not only disapproved of Seneca's works, but hated him personally. He refutes (*Institutes*, x., 1) that "vulgatam falso de me opinionem, qua damnare eum [sc. Senecam] et invisum quoque habere sum creditus." This naturally seemed to Petrarch a very exact analogy to the charges of jealousy brought against him.

[3] *Cum avo patreque meo vixit.* The reader is left to conjecture how intimate Dante and Petracco may have been when they lived together in Florence. Petrarch, in a reference to his father in *Sen.*, x., 2, would lead us to infer that he was born about 1252, twelve or thirteen years before Dante. There seems to be no means of deciding whether that statement or the one given in this letter, which makes Dante the older, is nearer the truth.

to me, towards this one, although it was readily procurable. The fact I admit, but I deny the motives which are urged by my enemies. At that time I too was devoting my powers to compositions in the vernacular; I was convinced that nothing could be finer, and had not yet learned to look higher. I feared, however, in view of the impressionableness of youth and its readiness to admire everything, that, if I should imbue myself with his or any other writer's verses, I might perhaps unconsciously and against my will come to be an imitator. In the ardour of youth this thought filled me with aversion. Such was my self-confidence and enthusiasm that I deemed my own powers quite sufficient, without any mortal aid, to produce an original style all my own, in the species of production upon which I was engaged. It is for others to judge whether I was right in this. But I must add that if anything should be discovered in my Italian writings resembling, or even identical with, what has been said by him or others, it cannot be attributed to secret or conscious imitation. This rock I have always endeavoured to avoid, especially in my writings in the vernacular, although it is possible that, either by accident or, as Cicero says, owing to similar ways of thinking, I may ignorantly have traversed the same path as others.[4] If you ever believe me, believe me now; accept this as the real explanation of my conduct. Nothing can be more strictly true; and if my modesty and sense of propriety did not seem to you sufficient to vouch for this, my youthful pride at any rate certainly might have explained it.

To-day, however, I have left these anxieties far behind, and, having done so, I am freed from my former apprehension, and can now unreservedly admire other writers, him above all. At that time I was submitting work of my own to the verdict of others, whereas now I am merely passing my own silent verdicts upon my fellows. I find that my opinion varies as regards all the rest, but in his case there can be no room for doubt; without hesitation I yield him the palm for skill in the use of the vulgar tongue. They lie, then, who assert that I carp at his renown; I, who probably understand better than the majority of these foolish and immoderate admirers of his what it is that merely tickles their ears, without their knowing why, but cannot penetrate their thick heads, because the avenues of intelligence are obstructed. They belong to the same class that Cicero brands in his *Rhetoric,* who "read fine orations or beautiful poems, and praise the orators or poets, and yet do not know what it is that has aroused their admiration, for they lack the ability to see where the thing is that most pleases them, or what it is, or how it is produced." If this happens with Demosthenes and Cicero, Homer and Virgil, among learned men and in the schools, how will it fare with our poet among the rude fellows who frequent the taverns and public squares?

As for me, far from scorning his work, I admire and love him, and in justice to myself I may venture to add that if he had been permitted to live until this time he would have found few friends more devoted to him than myself, provided, of course, that I had found his character as attractive as his genius. On the other hand, there are none to whom he would have been more obnoxious than these same silly admirers, who, in general, know equally little about what they praise and what they condemn, and who so mispronounce and lacerate his verses that they do him the greatest injury that a poet can suffer. I might even strive to the best of my powers to rescue him from this abuse, did not my own productions give me enough to think about. As it is, I can only give voice to my irritation, when I hear the common herd befouling with their stupid mouths the noble beauty of his lines.

Just here it may not be out of place to

---

[4] This matter of plagiarism is a subject to which Petrarch often reverts in his letters. He realised the difficulty of producing anything essentially new after the great works of classical antiquity.

say that this was not the least of the considerations which led me to give up a style of composition to which I devoted myself in my early years. I feared for my writings the same fate which I had seen overtake those of others, especially those of the poet of whom we are speaking. I could not in my own case look for more musical tongues or more flexible minds among the common people than I noted in the rendering of those authors whom long favour and habit have made popular in the theatres and public squares. That my apprehensions were not idle is clear from the fact that I am continually tortured by the tongues of the people, as they sing the few productions which I allowed to escape me in my youth. I indignantly reject and hate what I once loved; and day by day walk the streets with vexation and execrate my own talents. Everywhere a crowd of ignorant fellows, everywhere I find my Damoetas ready at the street corner "to murder with his screeching reed" my poor song.

However, I have already said more than enough concerning a trifling matter which I ought not to have taken so seriously, for this hour, which will never return, should have been devoted to other things. And yet your excuse did seem to me to have just a little in common with the accusations of these critics, some of whom are constantly asserting that I hate, some that I despise, this person,—whose name I have intentionally refrained to-day from mentioning, lest the mob, who catch up everything without understanding it, should cry out that I was defaming it. Others again claim that I am actuated by envy;—men who are jealous of me and my fame; for, although I scarcely am an object for envy, I yet have noticed late in life that there are those who entertain this feeling towards me, a thing that at one time I could not have believed possible. In answer to this charge of envy brought against me, I might reply that, many years ago, in the ardour of youth, and with an approving conscience, I ventured to assert, not in any ordinary man-

ner, but in a poem addressed to a certain illustrious personage, that I envied no man.[5] Suppose, though, that I am not worthy of belief. Still, even then, what probability is there that I should be jealous of a writer who devoted his whole life to those things which with me were but the flower and first-fruits of my youth? What to him was, if not his only occupation, certainly the supreme object of his life, to me was mere sport, a pastime, the first essay of my powers.[6]

What occasion is there here for rancour? What ground is there for even a suspicion of jealousy? When you say, in praising him, that he might have devoted himself to another kind of composition, had he wished, I heartily agree with you. I have the highest opinion of his ability, for it is obvious from what he has done that he would have succeeded in anything he might have chosen to undertake. But suppose that he had turned his powers in another direction, and successfully—what then? What would there be in that to make me jealous? Why should it not rather be a source of satisfaction to me? Who indeed could excite envy in me, who do not envy even Virgil?—unless perhaps I should be jealous of the hoarse applause which our poet enjoys from the tavern-keepers, fullers, butchers, and others of that class, who dishonour those whom they would praise. But, far from desiring such popular recognition, I congratulate myself, on the contrary, that, along with Virgil and Homer, I am free from it, inasmuch as I fully realise how little the plaudits of the unschooled multitude weigh with scholars. Should it be suggested that the citizen of Mantua is, when all is said, dearer to me than my fellow-citizen of Florence, I must urge that,

---

[5] This is probably a reference, as M. Develay suggests, to a metrical epistle addressed to Giacomo Colonna, the Bishop of Lombez, in which the following lines occur:

Nil usquam invideo, nullum ferventius odi,
Nullum despicio nisi me. . . .

[6] Namely, literary productions in the Italian tongue.

although I will not deny that jealousy does flourish most rankly between neighbours, the mere fact of common origin cannot by itself justify such an inference. Indeed the simple fact of our belonging to different generations would make this latter supposition absurd, for as one has elegantly said, who never speaks otherwise than elegantly, "The dead are neither hated nor envied."

You will accept my solemn affirmation that I delight in both the thought and style of our poet, nor do I ever refer to him except with the greatest admiration. It is true that I have sometimes said to those who wished to know precisely what I thought, that his style was unequal, for he rises to a higher plane of excellence in the vernacular than in poetry and prose.[7] But you will not deny this, nor will it, if rightly understood, carry with it any disparagement of his fame and glory. Who, indeed—I will not say at the present time, when eloquence has so long been mourned as dead, but at the time when it flourished most—who, I say, ever excelled in all its various branches? Witness Seneca's *Declamations!* [8] No one dreams of attributing inexhaustible versatility even to Cicero, Virgil, Sallust, or Plato. Who would lay claim to a degree of praise which must be denied even to such

genius? It is enough to have excelled in one kind of composition. This being true, let those be silent who attempt to twist my words into calumnies, and let those who have believed my calumniators read here, if they will, my opinion of them.

Having disposed thus of one matter which has been troubling me, I come now to a second. You thank me for my solicitude for your health. While you do this from courtesy, and in accordance with conventional usage, you well know that such acknowledgment is quite unnecessary. For who is ever thanked for his interest in himself, or his own affairs? and you, dear friend, are part and parcel of myself.

Although, next to virtue, friendship is the most sacred, the most God-like and divine thing in human intercourse, yet I think that it makes a difference whether one begins by loving or by being loved, and that those friendships should be more carefully fostered where we return love for love than where we simply receive it. I have been overwhelmed in a thousand instances by your kindness and friendly offices, but among them all there is one that I can never forget.

In days gone by, I was hurrying across central Italy in mid-winter; you hastened to greet me, not only with affectionate longings, which are the wings of the soul, but in person, impelled by a wondrous desire to behold one whom you had never yet seen,[9] but whom you were nevertheless resolved to love.

---

[7] Quod in vulgari eloquio, quam in carminibus aut prosa clarior atque altior assurgit. The literal form is retained in the rendering above, as Petrarch's very language is significant of his contempt for the Italian. Prose and verse could only be Latin.

[8] The work here referred to, which Petrarch supposed to be an inferior production of Seneca the Philosopher, is now attributed to his father, the Rhetor, of whose existence Petrarch was unaware.

[9] This would seem sufficient proof that Petrarch and Boccaccio first met on this occasion of Petrarch's visit to Florence.

Giambattista Vico

Discovery of the True Dante

THE *Divine Comedy* must be read from three points of approach: as a history of the period of barbarism in Italy, as a source of the fairest Tuscan speech, and as an example of sublime poetry.

With respect to the first of these, nature has disposed things thus: by reason of a development which is characteristic of the general mind of nations in the period when barbarism begins to be refined away, the poets of such periods sing truth: for barbarism itself is open and truthful precisely because lacking in that reflective mentality which, ill applied, is the mother of all falsehood. Thus in *The New Science* I called Homer the first historian of gentility; and this I further confirmed in my *Annotations* to his work, where I showed that he is quite other than the Homer of general acceptation. And surely the first historian of the Romans known to us was Ennius, who sang of the Carthaginian wars. By the same token our Dante was the first, or among the first, of Italian historians. He assumes the poet's role in his *Comedy* in so far as he tells us of the dead allocated to Inferno or Purgatory or Paradise, according to their deserts; and here he mingles truth and falsehood as a poet should if he is to be a Homer or an Ennius appropriate to our Christian religion with its teaching that rewards and punishments of our good and evil deeds are eternal rather than temporal ones. So that the allegories of Dante's poem are very like the reflections that a reader of history ought to make for himself: leading him to profit by the examples of others.

The second approach to the reading of Dante reveals him as a pure and copious fount of Tuscan speech. In this respect he has not yet been profitably studied, for it is still commonly supposed that Dante gathered together the speech of all the various Italian dialects. Which false notion must have taken root in the sixteenth century when learned men, beginning to cultivate the Tuscan language that had been spoken in Florence in the fourteenth century (the golden age of this language), observed in Dante a great number of locutions they had not found in other Tuscan writers, and, recognizing that many of these were, by good fortune, still current in other parts of Italy, concluded that Dante had gathered them thence into his *Comedy*. And this is exactly what happened when Homer was claimed as citizen by almost every people of Greece, since each one recognized in his poems their own native and still current locutions. But such a notion about Dante is false for two serious reasons. First, Florence, even in his times, must have shared the greater part of her speech forms with all the other cities of Italy: otherwise, the Italian tongue would not have had anything in common with that of Florence. And second, since the other cities in those unhappy times possessed no writers of the vulgar tongue (nor have developed any since), Dante's whole life would not have sufficed to learn the vulgar speech of so many communities and to get from them that abundance of forms he needed and employed to express his thought in the *Comedy*. And so what

"Discoverta del vero Dante, ovvero nuovi principi di critica dantesca, a proposito del commento d'un anonimo alla Commedia"; translated by the present editor from the text in G. B. Vico, *Opere*, edited by G. B. Nicolini, Milan, 1953. This essay is probably to be dated between 1728 and 1730.

our academicians of the Crusca should do is to set up a catalogue of such words and locutions and send it throughout Italy to the city folk of the lower classes (who preserve old customs and language better than do the nobles and courtiers), and to the peasants (who preserve such things better than do the lower-class townsmen), and in this way learn accurately how many and which forms were used, and with what meanings.

The third approach to Dante reveals a unique example of sublime poetry. It is the nature of sublime poetry that it cannot be learned by skill or craft. Homer is a sublimer poet than any who came after him—but he did not have any Longinus at his side to give him the rules of poetic sublimity. Nor can the great sources pointed out to us by Longinus be tasted except by such as have been destined by heaven to do so. The most sacred and deepest of these sources are two: first, loftiness of mind such as has no other concern than glory and immortality (rather does it despise and hold vile all those things that greedy, ambitious, soft, delicate, effeminate men commonly admire); and second, a mind informed by great and public virtues—and above all, by magnanimity and justice. The art-less Spartans, whose law forbade their knowing anything of letters, but whose young boys received the sublime education ordained by Lycurgus, uttered daily and under the most ordinary circumstances expressions that would adorn the work of the most illustrious tragic and heroic poets. But what was most peculiar to Dante's sublimity resulted from his having been born with the gift of genius in the era of Italy's expiring barbarism. For human talents are like those of the earth, which, if brought under cultivation after fallow centuries, produces at the outset fruits marvelous for their perfection, size, and abundance; but which, once tired from overmuch cultivation, yields only few, wizened, and small. And this is why, at the end of the barbarian period, there arose a Dante in sublime poetry, a Petrarch in delicate poetry, a Boccaccio in light and graceful prose: all three incomparable examples which we must by all means follow, but which we can by no means overtake. Whereas in our own highly cultivated era, such fair works of art as are being created may well raise in others the hope not merely of overtaking, but of surpassing them.

Voltaire

Dante

You wish to know Dante. The Italians call him *divine;* but he is a hidden divinity; virtually no one understands his oracles. He has commentators, it is true: probably one more reason why he remains incomprehensible. His reputation will always continue to be solid, because no one reads him. About twenty lines of his are widely known by heart; this spares people the trouble of examining the rest.

This divine Dante, they say, was a rather unfortunate man. Don't imagine that he was divine in his own time, or that he was a prophet in his own country. It is true that he was a prior—not a monastery prior, but a prior of Florence, which is to say one of its senators.

According to the word of his compatriots he was born in 1260. Bayle,[1] writing *currente calamo* at Rotterdam about four centuries after Dante, says he was born in 1265, and I esteem Bayle neither more nor less for having made an error of five years: the great point is to make no errors in taste or reasoning.[2]

The arts were just coming to birth in Dante's fatherland in his lifetime. Florence, like Athens, was full of wit, greatness, frivolity, unreliability, and factions. The *White* faction had one great point in its favor: it was named after the Signora Bianca. The opposing faction called itself the *Party of the Blacks*, with the object of more clearly distinguishing itself from the *Whites*. But these two factions were not enough for the Florentines. They had Guelphs and Ghibellines, too. Most of the Whites were Ghibellines, siding with the emperors, while the Blacks had a leaning for the Guelphs, who were attached to the popes.

All these factions loved liberty, and yet did what they could to destroy it. Pope Boniface VIII made up his mind to take advantage of these numerous cleavages in order to abolish the imperial power in Italy. He appointed Charles of Valois, brother of Philip the Fair, King of France, as his vicar in Tuscany. The vicar arrived well armed, expelled the Whites and Ghibellines, and made himself loathsome to the Blacks and Guelphs. Dante was a White and a Ghibelline;[3] he was among the first to be expelled, and his house was razed. One can guess from this what affection he felt all the rest of his life towards the house of France and the popes; still, they say that he made a journey to Paris; there became a theologian in order to avoid boredom, and took part vigorously in the disputes of the Schools. They add that the Emperor Henry VII never did anything for him in spite of his Ghibellinism; that he visited Frederic of Aragon, King of Sicily, and came away just as poor as before. He was then reduced to accepting the good graces of the Marquis of Malaspina and of Can Grande of Verona. The marquis and Can Grande failed to reward him; he died poor at Ravenna at the age of fifty-six. It was in these several places that he composed his comedy of hell, purgatory, and paradise;

[1] Pierre Bayle, author of the *Dictionnaire Historique.*

[2] Bayle was not mistaken. The reader is warned against any impulse to trust Voltaire's statements of fact in this article.

[3] Dante at this time was a White Guelph.

From Voltaire's *Dictionnaire Philosophique.* Translated by the editor, who has also supplied the notes.

people have pronounced this salmagundi to be a splendid poem.

Dante begins by finding a lion and a wolf at the entry of hell. Then, all at once, Virgil appears and offers him encouragement; and Virgil declares himself to have been born a Lombard. This last is exactly as though Homer were to announce that he had been born a Turk.[4] Virgil now offers to do Dante the honors of hell and purgatory, and to conduct him as far as St. Peter's gate; he acknowledges that he himself will be unable to enter there.

Charon presently ferries them both in his boat. Virgil tells how, shortly after his own arrival in hell, he saw there a powerful being who had come to collect the souls of Abel, Noah, Abraham, Moses, and David. As the two proceed on their way they come upon some very agreeable abodes in hell: in one of these are Homer, Horace, Ovid, and Lucan; in another they see Electra, Hector, Aeneas, Lucrece, Brutus, and the Turkish Saladin; in a third, Socrates, Plato, Hippocrates, and the Arab Averrhoës. At last the true hell comes into view, and here Pluto is found judging the condemned. The traveler now recognizes several cardinals, several popes, and a great number of Florentines. Is all this in the comic style? No. Is it all in heroic vein? No. Then what is the style of this poem? A bizarre one.

But it has in it some verses that come off so well and with such simplicity that they have not aged in four hundred years, and will never do so. In any case, a poem that puts popes into hell arouses a good deal of attention; and its commentators use up all the acumen of which they are capable in trying to determine the exact identity of each person Dante damned, without making a single error in a matter of such gravity.

They have founded an academic chair, a lectureship, in order to explain this classic writer. You will ask why the Inquisition

doesn't put a stop to it. I must answer that in Italy the Inquisition understands a joke; it well knows that pleasantries in verse can do no harm. You may judge, yourselves, by the following very free translation of a portion of the twenty-third canto, concerning one of the damned whom the poet knew personally. The sinner speaks as follows:[5]

Je m'appelais le comte de Guidon;
Je fus sur terre et soldat et poltron;
Puis m'enrôlai sous saint François d'Assise,
Afin qu'un jour le bout de son cordon
Me donnât place en la céleste Église;
Et j'y serais sans ce pape félon,
Qui m'ordonna de servir sa feintise,
Et me rendit aux griffes du démon.
Voici le fait. Quand j'étais sur la terre,
Vers Rimini je fis long-temps la guerre,
Moins, je l'avoue, en héros qu'en fripon.
L'art de fourber me fit un grand renom.
Mais quand mon chef eut porté poil grison,
Temps de retraite où convient la sagesse,
Le repentir vint ronger ma vieillesse,
Et j'eus recours à la confession.
O repentir tardif et peu durable!
Le bon Saint-Père en ce temps guerroyait,
Non le soudan, non le Turc intraitable,
Mais les chrétiens, qu'en vrai Turc il pillait.
Or, sans respect pour tiare et tonsure,
Pour saint François, son froc et sa ceinture,
Frère, dit-il, il me convient d'avoir
Incessamment Préneste en mon pouvoir.
Conseille-moi, cherche sous ton capuce
Quelque beau tour, quelque gentille astuce,
Pour ajouter en bref à mes états
Ce qui me tente et ne m'appartient pas.
J'ai les deux clefs du ciel en ma puissance.
De Célestin la dévote imprudence
S'en servit mal, et moi je sais ouvrir
Et refermer le ciel à mon plaisir.
Si tu me sers, ce ciel est ton partage.
Je le servis, et trop bien; dont j'enrage.
Il eut Préneste, et la mort me saisit.
Lors devers moi saint François descendit,
Comptant au ciel amener ma bonne ame;
Mais Belzébuth vint en poste, et lui dit:
Monsieur d'Assise, arrêtez: je réclame
Ce conseiller du Saint-Père, il est mien;
Bon saint François, que chacun ait le sien.

----

[4] All of Greece was part of the Ottoman Empire when Voltaire wrote.

[5] The editor thinks no explanation will be required for giving Voltaire's version of Inf. XXVII (not XXIII!), 67 ff., without tampering.

Lors tout penaud le bon-homme d'Assise
M'abandonnait au grand diable d'enfer.
Je lui criai: Monsieur de Lucifer,
Je suis un saint, voyez ma robe grise;
Je fus absous par le chef de l'Église.
J'aurai toujours, répondit le démon,
Un grand respect pour l'absolution:
On est lavé de ses vieilles sottises,
Pourvu qu'après autres ne soient commises.

J'ai fait souvent cette distinction
A tes pareils; et grace à l'Italie,
Le diable sait de la théologie.
Il dit, et rit: je ne répliquai rien
A Belzébuth; il raisonnait trop bien.
Lors il m'empoigne, et d'un bras roide et ferme
Il appliqua sur mon triste épiderme
Vingt coups de fouet, dont bien fort il me cuit:
Que Dieu le rende à Boniface huit!

Samuel Taylor Coleridge

Dante

As I remarked in a former Lecture on a different subject (for subjects the most diverse in literature have still their tangents), the Gothic character, and its good and evil fruits, appeared less in Italy than in any other part of European Christendom. There was accordingly much less romance, as that word is commonly understood; or, perhaps, more truly stated, there was romance instead of chivalry. In Italy, an earlier imitation of, and a more evident and intentional blending with, the Latin literature took place than elsewhere. The operation of the feudal system, too, was incalculably weaker, of that singular chain of independent interdependents, the principle of which was a confederacy for the preservation of individual, consistently with general, freedom. In short, Italy, in the time of Dante, was an afterbirth of eldest Greece, a renewal or a reflex of the old Italy under its kings and first Roman consuls, a net-work of free little republics, with the same domestic feuds, civil wars, and party spirit,—the same vices and virtues produced on a similarly narrow theatre,—the existing state of things being, as in all small democracies, under the working and direction of certain individuals, to whose will even the laws were swayed;—whilst at the same time the singular spectacle was exhibited amidst all this confusion of the flourishing of commerce, and the protection and encouragement of letters and arts. Never was the commercial spirit so well reconciled to the nobler principles of social polity as in Florence. It tended there to union and permanence and eleva-tion,—not as the overbalance of it in England is now doing, to dislocation, change and moral degradation. The intensest patriotism reigned in these communities, but confined and attached exclusively to the small locality of the patriot's birth and residence; whereas in the true Gothic feudalism, country was nothing but the preservation of personal independence. But then, on the other hand, as a counterbalance to these disuniting elements, there was in Dante's Italy, as in Greece, a much greater uniformity of religion common to all than amongst the northern nations.

Upon these hints the history of the republican aeras of ancient Greece and modern Italy ought to be written. There are three kinds or stages of historic narrative; —1. that of the annalist or chronicler, who deals merely in facts and events arranged in order of time, having no principle of selection, no plan of arrangement, and whose work properly constitutes a supplement to the poetical writings of romance or heroic legends:—2. that of the writer who takes his stand on some moral point, and selects a series of events for the express purpose of illustrating it, and in whose hands the narrative of the selected events is modified by the principle of selection;—as Thucydides, whose object was to describe the evils of democratic and aristocratic partizanships;—or Polybius, whose design was to show the social benefits resulting from the triumph and grandeur of Rome, in public institutions and military discipline;—or Tacitus, whose secret aim was to exhibit the pressure and corruptions of despotism;

From Coleridge's 1818 lecture on Dante, as reprinted in *Coleridge's Miscellaneous Criticism*, edited by T. M. Raysor, Cambridge, Mass., Harvard University Press, 1936.

—in all which writers and others like them, the ground-object of the historian colours with artificial lights the facts which he relates:—3. and which in idea is the grandest—the most truly founded in philosophy—there is the Herodotean history, which is not composed with reference to any particular causes, but attempts to describe human nature itself on a great scale as a portion of the drama of providence, the free will of man resisting the destiny of events,—for the individuals often succeeding against it, but for the race always yielding to it, and in the resistance itself invariably affording means towards the completion of the ultimate result. Mitford's history is a good and useful work; but in his zeal against democratic government, Mitford forgot, or never saw, that ancient Greece was not, nor ought ever to be considered, a permanent thing, but that it existed, in the disposition of providence, as a proclaimer of ideal truths, and that everlasting proclamation being made, that its functions were naturally at an end.

However, in the height of such a state of society in Italy, Dante was born and flourished; and was himself eminently a picture of the age in which he lived. But of more importance even than this, to a right understanding of Dante, is the consideration that the scholastic philosophy was then at its acme even in itself; but more especially in Italy, where it never prevailed so exclusively as northward of the Alps. It is impossible to understand the genius of Dante, and difficult to understand his poem, without some knowledge of the characters, studies, and writings of the schoolmen of the twelfth, thirteenth, and fourteenth centuries. For Dante was the living link between religion and philosophy; he philosophized the religion and christianized the philosophy of Italy; and, in this poetic union of religion and philosophy, he became the ground of transition into the mixed Platonism and Aristotelianism of the Schools, under which, by numerous minute articles of faith and ceremony, Christianity became

a craft of hair-splitting, and was ultimately degraded into a complete *fetisch* worship, divorced from philosophy, and made up of a faith without thought, and a credulity directed by passion. Afterwards, indeed, philosophy revived under condition of defending this very superstition; and, in so doing, it necessarily led the way to its subversion, and that in exact proportion to the influence of the philosophic schools. Hence it did its work most completely in Germany, then in England, next in France, then in Spain, least of all in Italy. We must, therefore, take the poetry of Dante as christianized, but without the further Gothic accession of proper chivalry. It was at a somewhat later period, that the importations from the East, through the Venetian commerce and the crusading armaments, exercised a peculiarly strong influence on Italy.

In studying Dante, therefore, we must consider carefully the differences produced, first, by allegory being substituted for polytheism; and secondly and mainly, by the opposition of Christianity to the spirit of pagan Greece, which receiving the very names of its gods from Egypt, soon deprived them of all that was universal. The Greeks changed the ideas into finites, and these finites into *anthropomorphi*, or forms of men. Hence their religion, their poetry, nay, their very pictures, became statuesque. With them the form was the end. The reverse of this was the natural effect of Christianity; in which finites, even the human form, must, in order to satisfy the mind, be brought into connexion with, and be in fact symbolical of, the infinite; and must be considered in some enduring, however shadowy and indistinct, point of view, as the vehicle or representative of moral truth.

Hence resulted two great effects; a combination of poetry with doctrine, and, by turning the mind inward on its own essence instead of letting it act only on its outward circumstances and communities, a combination of poetry with sentiment. And it is this inwardness or subjectivity, which principally and most fundamentally distinguishes all the classic from all the modern poetry. Compare the passage in the Iliad (Z. vi. 119–236) in which Diomed and Glaucus change arms,—

Χεῖράς τ’ ἀλλήλων λαβέτην καὶ πιστώσαντο—

They took each other by the hand, and pledged friendship—

with the scene in Ariosto (Orlando Furioso, c. i. st. 20–22), where Rinaldo and Ferrauto fight and afterwards make it up:—

Al Pagan la proposta non dispiacque:
Così fu differita la tenzone;
E tal tregua tra lor subito nacque,
Sì l’ odio e l’ ira va in oblivione,
Che ’l Pagano al partir dalle fresche acque
Non lasciò a piede il buon figliuol d’ Amone:
Con preghi invita, e al fin lo toglie in groppa,
E per l’ orme d’ Angelica galoppa.

Here Homer would have left it. But the Christian poet has his own feelings to express, and goes on:—

Oh gran bontà de’ cavalieri antiqui!
Eran rivali, eran di fè diversi,
E si sentían degli aspri colpi iniqui
Per tutta la persona anco dolersi;
E pur per selve oscure e calli obbliqui
Insieme van senza sospetto aversi!

And here you will observe, that the reaction of Ariosto’s own feelings on the image or act is more fore-grounded (to use a painter’s phrase) than the image or act itself.[1]

The two different modes in which the imagination is acted on by the ancient and modern poetry, may be illustrated by the parallel effects caused by the contemplation of the Greek or Roman-Greek architecture, compared with the Gothic. In the Pantheon, the whole is perceived in a perceived harmony with the parts which compose it;

[1] Cf. this paragraph with its evident source in Schiller’s “Of Naïve and Sentimental Poetry.”

and generally you will remember that where the parts preserve any distinct individuality, there simple beauty, or beauty simply, arises; but where the parts melt undistinguished into the whole, there majestic beauty, or majesty, is the result. In York Minster, the parts, the grotesques, are in themselves very sharply distinct and separate, and this distinction and separation of the parts is counterbalanced only by the multitude and variety of those parts, by which the attention is bewildered;—whilst the whole, or that there is a whole produced, is altogether a feeling in which the several thousand distinct impressions lose themselves as in a universal solvent. Hence in a Gothic cathedral, as in a prospect from a mountain’s top, there is, indeed, a unity, an awful oneness;—but it is, because all distinction evades the eye. And just such is the distinction between the Antigone of Sophocles and the Hamlet of Shakespeare.

The Divina Commedia is a system of moral, political, and theological truths, with arbitrary personal exemplifications, which are not, in my opinion, allegorical. I do not even feel convinced that the punishments in the Inferno are strictly allegorical. I rather take them to have been in Dante’s mind *quasi*-allegorical, or conceived in analogy to pure allegory.

I have said, that a combination of poetry with doctrines, is one of the characteristics of the Christian muse; but I think Dante has not succeeded in effecting this combination nearly so well as Milton.

This comparative failure of Dante, as also some other peculiarities of his mind, *in malam partem*, must be immediately attributed to the state of North Italy in his time, which is vividly represented in Dante’s life; a state of intense democratical partizanship, in which an exaggerated importance was attached to individuals, and which whilst it afforded a vast field for the intellect, opened also a boundless arena for the passions, and in which envy, jealousy, hatred, and other malignant feelings, could and did assume the form of patriotism, even to the individual's own conscience.

All this common, and, as it were, natural partizanship was aggravated and coloured by the Guelf and Ghibelline factions; and, in part explanation of Dante's adherence to the latter, you must particularly remark, that the Pope had recently territorialized his authority to a great extent, and that this increase of territorial power in the church, was by no means the same beneficial movement for the citizens of free republics, as the parallel advance in other countries was for those who groaned as vassals under the oppression of the circumjacent baronial castles.

By way of preparation to a satisfactory perusal of the Divina Commedia, I will now proceed to state what I consider to be Dante's chief excellence as a poet. And I begin with

I. Style—the vividness, logical connexion, strength and energy of which cannot be surpassed. In this I think Dante superior to Milton; and his style is accordingly more imitable than Milton's, and does to this day exercise a greater influence on the literature of his country. You cannot read Dante without feeling a gush of manliness of thought within you. Dante was very sensible of his own excellence in this particular, and speaks of poets as guardians of the vast armory of language, which is the intermediate something between matter and spirit:—

Or se' tu quel Virgilio, e quella fonte,
Che spande di parlar sì largo fiume?
Risposi lui con vergognosa fronte.
O degli altri poeti onore e lume,
Vagliami 'l lungo studio e 'l grande amore,
Che m' han fatto cercar lo tuo volume.
Tu se' lo mio maestro, e 'l mio autore:
Tu se' solo colui, da cu' io tolsi
Lo bello stile, che m' ha fatto onore.
Inf., c. 1. v. 79.

"And art thou then that Virgil, that well-
spring,
From which such copious floods of eloquence

Have issued?" I, with front abash'd, replied:
"Glory and light of all the tuneful train!
May it avail me, that I long with zeal
Have sought thy volume, and with love immense
Have conn'd it o'er. My master, thou, and guide!
Thou he from whom alone I have deriv'd
That style, which for its beauty into fame
Exalts me."
CARY.

Indeed there was a passion and a miracle of words in the twelfth and thirteenth centuries, after the long slumber of language in barbarism, which gave an almost romantic character, a virtuous quality and power, to what was read in a book, independently of the thoughts or images contained in it. This feeling is very often perceptible in Dante.

II. The Images in Dante are not only taken from obvious nature, and are all intelligible to all, but are ever conjoined with the universal feeling received from nature, and therefore affect the general feelings of all men. And in this respect, Dante's excellence is very great, and may be contrasted with the idiosyncracies of some meritorious modern poets, who attempt an eruditeness, the result of particular feelings. Consider the simplicity, I may say plainness, of the following simile, and how differently we should in all probability deal with it at the present day:

Quale i fioretti dal notturno gelo
Chinati e chiusi, poi che 'l sol gl' imbianca,
Si drizzan tutti aperti in loro stelo,—
Tal mi fec' io di mia virtute stanca:
Inf., c. 2. v. 127.

As florets, by the frosty air of night
Bent down and clos'd, when day has blanch'd
their leaves,
Rise all unfolded on their spiry stems,—
So was my fainting vigour new restor'd.
CARY.

III. Consider the wonderful profoundness of the whole third canto of the Inferno; and especially of the inscription over Hell gate:

Per me si va, &c.—

which can only be explained by a meditation on the true nature of religion; that is, —reason *plus* the understanding. I say profoundness rather than sublimity; for Dante does not so much elevate your thoughts as send them down deeper. In this canto all the images are distinct, and even vividly distinct; but there is a total impression of infinity; the wholeness is not in vision or conception, but in an inner feeling of totality, and absolute being.

Ugo Foscolo

A Parallel between Dante and Petrarch

L'un disposto a patire e l'altro a fare.
DANTE, Purg. c. XXV

I. The excess of erudition in the age of Leo the Tenth [1] carried the refinements of criticism so far as even to prefer elegance of taste to boldness of genius. The laws of the Italian language were thus deduced, and the models of poetry selected exclusively from the works of Petrarch; who being then proclaimed superior to Dante, the sentence remained, until our times, unreversed. Petrarch himself mingles Dante indiscriminately with others eclipsed by his own fame—

Ma ben ti prego, che in la terza spera,
Guitton saluti, e Messer Cino, e Dante,
Franceschin nostro, e tutta quella schiera.

Così or quinci, or quindi rimirando
Vidi in una fiorita e verde piaggia
Gente che d' Amor givan ragionando.

Ecco Dante, e Beatrice: ecco Selvaggia,
Ecco Cin da Pistoja; Guitton d' Arezzo;
Ecco i due Guidi che già furo in prezzo;
Onesto Bolognese, e i Siciliani.—
Trionf. c. 4.

Salute, I pray thee, in the sphere of love,
Guitton, my master Cino, Dante too,
Our Franceschin, all that blest band above.——
Thus while my gazing eyes around me rove,
I saw upon a slope of flowery green
Many that held their sweet discourse of love:
Here Dante and his Beatrice, there were seen
Selvaggia and Cino of Pistoja; there
Guitton the Aretine; and the high-priz'd pair,

The Guidi; and Onesto these among,
And all the masters of Sicilian song.
MILMAN.

Boccaccio, discouraged by the reputation of these two great masters, determined to burn his own poetry. Petrarch diverted him from this purpose, writing with a tone of humility somewhat inconsistent with the character of a man who was not naturally a hypocrite. "You are a philosopher and a christian," says he, "and yet you are discontented with yourself for not being an illustrious poet! Since *another* has occupied the *first* place, be satisfied with the *second,* and I will take the *third.*" [2] Boccaccio, perceiving the irony and the allusion, sent Dante's poem to Petrarch, and intreated that "he would not disdain to read the work of a great man, from whom exile and death, while he was still in the vigour of life, had snatched the laurel." [3]—"Read it, I conjure you; your genius reaches to the heavens, and your glory extends beyond the earth: but reflect that Dante is our fellow-citizen; that he has shewn all the force of our language; that his life was unfortunate; that he undertook and suffered every thing for glory; and that he is still pursued by calumny, and by envy, in the grave. If you praise him, you will do honour to him—you will do honour to yourself—you will do honour to Italy, of which you are the greatest glory and the only hope."

[1] Pope Leo X (Giovanni de' Medici) held office 1513–1521.—Ed.

[2] Senil. Lib. 5. Ep. 2. et 3.
[3] Nec tibi sit durum versus vidisse poetae Exsulis. ——

Reprinted, with omission of several brief passages and quotations, from U. Foscolo, *Essays on Petrarch,* London, John Murray, 1823. Original text in English.

II. Petrarch, in his answer, is angry that he can be considered jealous of the celebrity of a poet "whose language is coarse, though his conceptions are lofty"— "You must hold him in veneration and in gratitude, as the first light of your education, whilst I never saw him but once, at a distance, or rather he was pointed out to me, while I was still in my childhood. He was exiled on the same day with my father, who submitted to his misfortunes, and devoted himself solely to the care of his children. The other, on the contrary, resisted, followed the path which he had chosen, thought only of glory, and neglected every thing else. If he were still alive, and if his character were as congenial to mine as his genius is, he would not have a better friend than me." [4]—This letter lengthened out by contradictions, ambiguities, and indirect apologies, points out the individual by circumlocutions, as if the name was withheld through caution or through awe. Some maintain that Dante is not referred to; [5] but the authentic list [6] still existing, of the Florentines banished on the 27th of January 1302, contains the names of Dante and the father of Petrarch, and that of no other individual to whom it is possible to apply any one of the circumstances mentioned in the letter, whilst each, and the whole of them, apply strictly to Dante.

III. These two founders of Italian literature were gifted with a very different genius, pursued different plans, established two different languages and schools of poetry, and have exercised till the present time a very different influence. Instead of selecting, as Petrarch does, the most elegant and melodious words and phrases, Dante often creates a new language, and summons all the various dialects of Italy to furnish him with combinations that might represent, not only the sublime and beautiful, but even the commonest scenes of nature; all the wild conceptions of his fancy; the most abstract theories of philosophy, and the most abstruse mysteries of religion. A simple idea, a vulgar idiom, takes a different colour and a different spirit from their pen. The conflict of opposite purposes *thrills in the heart* of Petrarch, and *battles in the brain* of Dante—

> Nè sì nè no nel cor dentro mi suona.—PETR.
> Che sì e no nel capo mi tenzona.—DANTE.
> At war 'twixt will and will not.—SHAKSPEARE.

Tasso expressed it with that dignity from which he never departs—

> In gran tempesta di pensieri ondeggia.

Yet not only does this betray an imitation of the *magno curarum fluctuat aestu* of Virgil; but Tasso, by dreading the energy of the idiom *sì e no*, lost, as he does too often, the graceful effect produced by ennobling a vulgar phrase—an artifice which, however, in the pastoral of Aminta he has most successfully employed. His notion of epic style was so refined, that while he regarded Dante "as the greatest poet of Italy," he often asserted, "had he not sacrificed dignity and elegance, he would have been the first of the world."—No doubt Dante sometimes sacrificed even decorum and perspicuity; but it was always to impart more fidelity to his pictures, or more depth to his reflections. He says to himself—

> Parla, e sie breve e arguto.—
> Speak; and be brief, be subtile in thy words.

He says to his reader—

> Or ti riman, lettor, sovra 'l tuo banco,
> Dietro pensando a ciò, che si preliba,
> S' esser vuoi lieto assai prima, che stanco.
> *Messo t' ho innanzi; omai per te ti ciba.*

> Now rest thee, reader, on thy bench, and muse
> Anticipative of the feast to come;
> So shall delight make thee not feel thy toil.
> *Lo! I have set before thee; for thyself*
> *Feed now.*
>
> CARY'S Transl.

---

[4] Petr. Epist. edit. Ginevr. an. 1601. p. 445.
[5] Tiraboschi, Storia della Let. Ital. vol. 9. lib. 3. cap. 2. sect. 10.
[6] Muratori, Script. Rer. Ital. vol. 10. p. 501.

IV. As to their versification, Petrarch attained the main object of erotic poetry; which is, to produce a constant musical flow in strains inspired by the sweetest of human passions. Dante's harmony is less melodious, but is frequently the result of more powerful art—

S' i' avessi le rime e aspre e chiocce,
Come si converebbe al tristo buco,
Sovra 'l qual pontan tutte l' altre rocce,
I' premerei di mio concetto il suco
Più pienamente: ma perch' i' non l' abbo,
Non senza tema a dicer mi conduco:
Che non è impresa da pigliare a gabbo,
Descriver fondo a tutto l' universo,
Nè da lingua, che chiami mamma o babbo.
Ma quelle donne ajutino 'l mio verso,
Ch' ajutaro Anfione a chiuder Tebe,
Sì che dal fatto il dir non sia diverso.

Oh! had I rough hoarse thunder in my verse,
To match this gulph of woe on all sides round
O'erbrow'd by rocks, then dreadfully should
   roar
The mighty torrent of my song: such powers
I boast not; but with shuddering awe attempt
The solemn theme. The world's extremest depth
Requires no infant babbling, but the choir
Of tuneful virgins to assist my strain,
By whose symphonious aid Amphion raised
The Theban walls,—but truth shall guide my
   tongue.

N. HOWARD'S Transl.[7]

Here the poet evidently hints that to give colour and strength to ideas by the sound of words, is one of the necessary requisites of the art. The six first lines are made rough by a succession of consonants. But when he describes a quite different sub-ject, the words are more flowing with vowels—

O anime affannate,
Venite a noi parlar, s' altri nol niega.
   Quali colombe dal desio chiamate,
Con l' ali aperte e ferme al dolce nido,
Volan per l' aer dal voler portate.

"O wearied spirits! come, and hold discourse
With us, if by none else restrain'd." As doves
By fond desire invited, on wide wings
And firm, to their sweet nests returning home,
Cleave the air, wafted by their will along.

CARY'S Transl.

This translator frequently contravenes the position of his author, who, chiefly depending upon the effect of his versification, says, that "nothing harmonized by musical enchainment, can be transmuted from one tongue into another, without destroying all its sweetness and harmony."[8]—The plan of Dante's poem required that he should pass from picture to picture, from passion to passion. He varies the tone in the different scenes of his journey as rapidly as the crowd of spectres flitted before his eyes; and he adapts the syllables and the cadences of each line, in such an artful manner as to give energy, by the change of his numbers, to those images which he intended to represent. For in the most harmonious lines, there is no poetry, whenever they fail to excite that glow of rapture, that exquisite thrill of delight, which arises from the easy and simultaneous agitation of all our faculties—this the poet achieves by powerful use of imagery. . . .

VI. Petrarch's images seem to be exquisitely finished by a very delicate pencil: they delight the eye rather by their colouring than by their forms. Those of Dante are the bold and prominent figures of an *alto rilievo*, which, it seems, we might almost touch, and of which the imagination readily supplies those parts that are hidden from the view. The commonplace thought of the vanity of human renown is thus expressed by Petrarch—

---

[7] The translation here given by Foscolo so obscures the great validity of his critical point that we venture to offer the following literal rendering: *If I had rhymes rough and bitter such as would match the dismal hole above which hang all the other rocks, I should more fully press out the juice of my conception; but since I have not, not without fear do I bring myself to speak: for to describe the bottom of the whole universe is not to be undertaken in play, nor by a tongue that cries mamma and papa. But may those Ladies aid my verse who aided Amphion to close in Thebes—so that my telling be not different from the fact.*—Ed.

[8] Dante, Convito.

O ciechi, il tanto affaticar che giova?
Tutti tornate alla gran madre antica,
E il vostro nome appena si ritrova.

O blind of intellect! of what avail
Are your long toils in this sublunar vale?

Tell, ye benighted souls! what gains accrue
From the sad task, which ceaseless ye pursue?
Ye soon must mingle with the dust ye tread;
And scarce your name upon a stone be read.

BOYD'S Transl.

and by Dante,

La vostra nominanza è color d'erba,
Che viene e va; e quei la discolora
Per cui vien fuori della terra acerba.

Your mortal fame is like the grass whose hue
Doth come and go; by the same sun decay'd,
From which it life, and health, and freshness
drew.

MERIVALE.

The three lines of Petrarch have the great merit of being more spirited, and of conveying more readily the image of the earth swallowing up the bodies and names of all men; but those of Dante, in spite of their stern profundity, have the still greater merit of leading us on to ideas to which we should not ourselves have reached. Whilst he reminds us, that time, which is necessary for the consummation of all human glory, ultimately destroys it, the changing colour of grass presents the revolutions of ages, as the natural occurrence of a few moments. . . . Again, instead of the agency of time, Dante employs the agency of the sun; because, conveying to us a less metaphysical idea, and being an object more palpable to the senses, it abounds with more glorious and evident images, and fills us with greater wonder and admiration. Its application is more logical also, since every notion which we have of time, consists in the measure of it, which is afforded by the periodical revolutions of the sun.

VII. With respect to the different pleasure these two poets afford, it has been already remarked, that Petrarch calls forth the sweetest sympathies, and awakens the deepest emotions, of the heart: and whether they be of a sad, or of a lively cast, we eagerly wish for them, because, the more they agitate us, the more strongly they quicken our consciousness of existence. Still, as we are perpetually striving against pain, and hurried on in the constant pursuit of pleasure, our hearts would sink under their own agitations, were they abandoned by the dreams of imagination, with which we are providentially gifted to enlarge our stock of happiness, and to gild with bright illusions the sad realities of life. Great writers alone can so control the imagination, as to make it incapable of distinguishing these illusions from the reality. If, in a poem, the ideal and fanciful predominate, we may indeed be surprised for a moment, but can never be brought to feel for objects which either have no existence, or are too far removed from our common nature—and on the other hand, if poetry dwell too much on realities, we soon grow weary; for we see them wherever we turn; they sadden each minute of our existence; they disgust us ever, because we know them even to satiety:—again, if reality and fiction be not intimately blended into one whole, they mutually oppose and destroy one another. Petrarch does not afford many instances of so happy a combination of truth with fiction, as when he describes Laura's features immediately after expiring—

Pallida no, ma più che neve bianca—
Parea posar come persona stanca.

Quasi un dolce dormir ne' suoi begli occhi,
Sendo lo spirto già da lei diviso—
Morte bella parea nel suo bel viso.

No earthy hue her pallid cheek display'd,
But the pure snow—
Like one recumbent from her toils she lay,
Losing in sleep the labours of the day—
And from her parting soul an heavenly trace
Seem'd yet to play upon her lifeless face,
Where death enamour'd sate, and smiled with
angel grace.

BOYD'S Transl.

Had the translator kept closer in the last line to the original words, "Death seemed beautiful on the lovely features of Laura," he would have conveyed a higher and yet more credible notion of her beauty, and insensibly changed, into an agreeable sensation, the horror with which we regard a corpse. But "Death sitting enamour'd in Laura's face," exhibits no distinct image, unless it be that of the allegorical form of Death transmuted into an angel sitting upon the face of a woman—which affords a striking exemplification of the absurdities arising from the unskilful mixture of truth with fiction.

VIII. Petrarch often surrounds the reality with ideal decorations so luxuriantly, that while we gaze at his images they disappear. . . . Dante selects the beauties that lie scattered throughout created Nature, and embodies them in one single subject. The artists who combined in the Apollo of Belvidere, and the Venus de' Medicis, the various beauties observed in different individuals, produced forms, which, though strictly human, have an air of perfection not to be met with upon the earth: however, when contemplating them, we are led insensibly to indulge in the illusion, that mankind may possess such heavenly beauty—

Stiamo, Amor, a veder la gloria nostra,
Cose sopra natura altere e nove:
Vedi ben quanta in lei dolcezza piove;
Vedi lume che 'l cielo in terra mostra;
    Vedi quant' arte indora, e imperla, e innostra
L' abito eletto, e mai non visto altrove,
Che dolcemente i piedi, e gli occhi move
Per questa di bei colli ombrosa chiostra.
    L'erbetta verde, e i fior di color mille
Sparsi sotto quell' elce antiqua e negra,
Pregan pur che 'l bel pie' li prema o tocchi;
    E 'l ciel di vaghe e lucide faville
S' accende intorno, e' n vista si rallegra
D' esser fatto seren da sì begli occhi.

Here stand we, Love, our glory to behold—
    How, passing nature, lovely, high, and rare!
    Behold! what showers of sweetness falling
        there!

What floods of light by heav'n to earth unroll'd!
How shine her robes, in purple, pearls, and gold
    So richly wrought, with skill beyond compare!
    How glance her feet!—her beaming eyes how
        fair
Through the dark cloister which these hills enfold!
The verdant turf, and flowers of thousand hues
    Beneath yon oak's old canopy of state,
    Spring round her feet to pay their amorous
        duty.
The heavens, in joyful reverence, cannot choose
    But light up all their fires, to celebrate
    Her praise, whose presence charms their awful
        beauty.

MERIVALE.

This description makes us long to find such a woman in the world; but while we admire the poet, and envy him the bliss of his amorous transports, we cannot but perceive that the flowers "that courted the tread of her foot," the sky "that grew more beautiful in her presence," the atmosphere "that borrowed new splendour from her eyes," are mere visions which tempt us to embark with him in the pursuit of an unattainable chimaera. We are induced to think, that Laura must have been endowed with more than human loveliness, since she was able to kindle her lover's imagination to such a degree of enthusiasm, as to cause him to adopt such fantastic illusions, and we conceive the extremity of his passion; but cannot share his amorous ecstasies for a beauty which we never beheld and never shall behold.

IX. On the contrary, the beautiful maiden seen afar off by Dante, in a landscape of the terrestrial paradise, instead of appearing an imaginary being, seems to unite in herself all the attractions which are found in those lovely creatures we sometimes meet, whom we grieve to lose sight of, and to whom fancy is perpetually recurring—the poet's picture recalls the original more distinctly to our memory, and enshrines it in our imagination—

Una donna soletta, che si gia
Cantando ed iscegliendo fior da fiore,

Ond' era pinta tutta la sua via.
  "Deh bella donna, ch' a' raggi d' amore
Ti scaldi, s' io vo' credere a' sembianti,
Che soglion' esser testimon del cuore,
  Vengati voglia di trarreti avanti,"
Diss' io a lei, "verso questa riviera,
Tanto ch' io possa intender che tu canti."
  Come si volge con le piante strette
A terra, e intra sè, donna che balli,
E piede innanzi piede a pena mette,
  Volsesi 'n su' vermigli ed in su' gialli
Fioretti, verso me, non altrimenti,
Che vergine, che gli occhi onesti avvalli;
  E fece i prieghi miei esser contenti,
Sì appressando sè, che 'l dolce suono
Veniva a me co' suoi intendimenti.

                              I beheld
A lady all alone, who, singing, went,
And culling flower from flower, wherewith her
    way
Was all o'er painted. "Lady beautiful!
Thou, who (if looks, that use to speak the heart,
Are worthy of our trust) with love's own beam
Dost warm thee," thus to her my speech I
    fram'd;
"Ah! please thee hither tow'rds the streamlet
    bend
Thy steps so near, that I may list thy song."—
  As when a lady, turning in the dance,
Doth foot it featly, and advances scarce
One step before the other to the ground;
Over the yellow and vermillion flowers
Thus turn'd she at my suit, most maiden-like,
Veiling her sober eyes: and came so near,
That I distinctly caught the dulcet sound.
                              CARY's Transl.

Such is the amazing power with which
Dante mingles the realities of nature with
ideal accessories, that he creates an illusion which no subsequent reflection is able
to dissipate. All that grace and beauty, that
warmth and light of love, that vivacity and
cheerfulness of youth, that hallowed modesty of a virgin, which we observe, though
separately and intermixed with defects, in
different persons, are here concentrated into one alone; whilst her song, her dance,
and her gathering of flowers, give life, and
charm, and motion, to the picture.—To
judge fairly between these two poets, it appears, that Petrarch excels in awakening

the heart to a deep feeling of its existence;
and Dante, in leading the imagination to
add to the interest and novelty of nature.
Probably a genius never existed, that enjoyed these two powers at once in a pre-
eminent degree.

X. Having both worked upon plans suited to their respective talents, the result has
been two kinds of poetry, productive of opposite moral effects. Petrarch makes us see
every thing through the medium of one
predominant passion, habituates us to indulge in those propensities which by keep-
ing the heart in perpetual disquietude, par-
alyze intellectual exertion—entice us into
a morbid indulgence of our feelings, and
withdraw us from active life. Dante, like
all primitive poets, is the historian of the
manners of his age, the prophet of his
country, and the painter of mankind; and
calls into action all the faculties of our
soul to reflect on all the vicissitudes of the
world. He describes all passions, all actions—the charm and the horror of the
most different scenes. He places men in
the despair of Hell, in the hope of Purgatory, and in the blessedness of Paradise.
He observes them in youth, in manhood,
and in old age. He has brought together
those of both sexes, of all religions, of all
occupations, of different nations, and ages;
yet he never takes them in masses—he always presents them as individuals; speaks
to every one of them, studies their
words, and watches their countenances.—
"I found," says he, in a letter to Can della
Scala, "the original of my Hell, in the
earth we inhabit." While describing the
realms of death, he catches at every oppor-
tunity to bring us back to the occupations
and affections of the living world. Perceiving the sun about to quit our hemisphere,
he breaks out into—

    Era già l' ora, che volge 'l desio
  A' naviganti, e intenerisce il core
  Lo dì, ch' han detto a' dolci amici Addio;
    E che lo nuovo peregrin d' amore
  Punge, se ode squilla di lontano,
  Che paja 'l giorno pianger, che si muore.

'Twas now the hour when fond desire renews
 To him who wanders o'er the pathless main,
Raising unbidden tears, the last adieus
 Of tender friends, whom fancy shapes again;
When the late parted pilgrim thrills with
 thought
 Of his lov'd home, if o'er the distant plain,
Perchance, his ears the village chimes have
 caught,
 Seeming to mourn the close of dying day.
MERIVALE.

There is a passage very like this in Apollonius Rhodius, whose many beauties, so admired in the imitations of Virgil, are seldom sought for in the original.—

Night then brought darkness o'er the earth:
 at sea
The mariners their eyes from shipboard raised,
Fix'd on the star Orion, and the Bear.
The traveller, and the keeper of the gate,
Rock'd with desire of sleep; and slumber now
Fell heavy on some mother, who had wept
Her children in the grave.
ELTON'S Transl.

By digressions similar to this, introduced without apparent art or effort, Dante interests us for all mankind; whilst Petrarch, being interested only about himself, alludes to men at sea at eventide, only to excite greater compassion for his own sufferings—

E i naviganti in qualche chiusa valle
Gettan le membra, poi che 'l sol s'asconde,
Sul duro legno e sotto l' aspre gonne:
Ma io; perchè s' attuffi in mezzo l'onde,
E lassi Ispagna dietro alle sue spalle,
E Granata e Marocco e le Colonne,
E gli uomini e le donne
E 'l mondo, e gli animali
Acquetino i lor mali,
Fine non pongo al mio ostinato affanno:
E duolmi ch' ogni giorno arroge al danno;
Ch' i' son già pur crescendo in questa voglia
Ben presso al decim' anno,
Nè poss' indovinar chi me ne scioglia.

And in some shelter'd bay, at evening's close,
The mariners their rude coats round them fold,
Stretch'd on the rugged plank in deep repose:
But I, though Phoebus sink into the main

And leave Granada wrapt in night, with Spain,
Morocco, and the Pillars famed of old,
Though all of human kind
And every creature blest
All hush their ills to rest,
No end to my unceasing sorrows find;
And still the sad account swells day by day;
For since these thoughts on my lorn spirit prey,
I see the tenth year roll,
Nor hope for freedom springs in my desponding
 soul.
LADY DACRE.

Hence Petrarch's poetry wraps us in an idle melancholy, in the softest and sweetest visions, in the error of depending upon others' affection, and leads us vainly to run after perfect happiness, until we plunge headlong into that despair which ensues,

When Hope has fled affrighted from thy face,
And giant Sorrow fills the empty place.

Still those who meet with this fate are comparatively very few, while far the greater number only learn from sentimental reading how to work more successfully upon impassioned minds, or to spread over vice a thicker cloak of hypocrisy. The number of Petrarch's imitators in Italy may be ascribed to the example of those Church dignitaries and learned men, who, to justify their commerce with the other sex, borrowed the language of Platonic love from his poetry. It is also admirably calculated for a Jesuits' college, since it inspires devotion, mysticism, and retirement, and enervates the minds of youth. But since the late revolutions have stirred up other passions, and a different system of education has been established, Petrarch's followers have rapidly diminished; and those of Dante have written poems more suited to rouse the public spirit of Italy. Dante applied his poetry to the vicissitudes of his own time, when liberty was making her dying struggle against tyranny; and he descended to the tomb with the last heroes of the middle age. Petrarch lived amongst those who prepared the inglorious heritage of servitude for the next fifteen generations.

XI. It was about the decline of Dante's life that the constitutions of the Italian States underwent a total and almost universal change, in consequence of which a new character was suddenly assumed by men, manners, literature, and religion. It was then that the Popes and Emperors, by residing out of Italy, abandoned her to factions, which having fought for independence or for power, continued to tear themselves to pieces through animosity, until they reduced their country to such a state of exhaustion, as to make it an easy prey to demagogues, to despots, and to foreigners. The Guelphs were no longer sanctioned by the Church, in their struggle for popular rights against the feudatories of the empire. The Ghibellines no longer allied themselves to the Emperors to preserve their privileges as great proprietors. Florence, and other small republics, after extirpating their nobles, were governed by merchants, who, having neither ancestors to imitate, nor generosity of sentiment, nor a military education, carried on their intestine feuds by calumny and confiscation. Afraid of a domestic dictatorship, they opposed their external enemies by foreign leaders of mercenary troops, often composed of adventurers and vagabonds from every country, who plundered friends and foes alike, exasperated the discords, and polluted the morals, of the nation. French princes reigned at Naples; and to extend their influence over the south of Italy, destroyed the very shadow of the imperial authority there, by stimulating the Guelphs to all the extravagances of democracy. Meanwhile the nobles who upheld the Ghibelline faction in the north of Italy, being possessed of the wealth and strength of the country, continued to wage incessant civil wars, until they, with their towns and their vassals, were all subjected to the military sway of the victorious leaders, who were often murdered by their own soldiers, and oftener by the heirs apparent of their power. Venice alone, being surrounded by the sea, and consequently exempted from the danger of invasion, and from the necessity of confiding her armies to a single patrician, enjoyed an established form of government. Nevertheless, to preserve and extend her colonies and her commerce, she carried on, in the Mediterranean, a destructive contest with other maritime cities. The Genoese having lost their principal fleet, bartered their liberties with the tyrants of Lombardy, in exchange for assistance. They were thus enabled to gratify their hatred, and defeat the Venetians, who to repeat their attacks exhausted their resources; and both states now fought less for interest, than revenge. It was then that Petrarch's exhortations to peace were so haughtily answered by the Doge Andrea Dandolo. Thus the Italians, though then the arbiters of the seas, weakened themselves to such a degree, by their blind animosities, that, in the ensuing century, Columbus was compelled to beg the aid of foreign princes, to open that path of navigation which has since utterly destroyed the commercial grandeur of Italy.

XII. Meanwhile the Popes and Cardinals, vigilantly watched at Avignon, were sometimes the forced, and often the voluntary, abettors of French policy. The German Princes, beginning to despise the Papal excommunication, refused either to elect Emperors patronized by the Holy See, or to lead forth their subjects to the conquest of the Holy Land, a device, by which from the beginning of the twelfth to the end of the thirteenth century, all the armies of Europe had actually been at the disposal of the Popes. The wild and enterprising fanaticism of religion having thus ceased with the crusades, dwindled into a gloomy and suspicious superstition: new articles of belief brought from the east, gave birth to new Christian sects: the circulation of the classics, the diffusion of a taste for Greek metaphysics, and the Aristotelian materialism, spread through Europe by the writings of Averroës, induced some of Dante's and Petrarch's contemporaries to doubt even the existence of God. It was then deemed expedient to maintain both the authority of the Gospel, and the temporal influence of the Church, by the arbitrary and mysterious laws of the Holy Inquisition. Several of the Popes who filled the chair of St. Peter during the life of Dante, had been originally friars of the order of St. Dominick, the founder of that tribunal; and their successors, in the age of Petrarch, were prelates of France, either corrupted by luxury, or devoted to the interest of their country. The terror which had been propagated by the Dominicans, was followed by the sale of indulgences, and the celebration of the jubilees, instituted about this time by Boniface VIII. As the sovereign pontiffs were no longer allowed to employ in political projects the riches which they derived from their religious ascendancy, ambition yielded to covetousness; and they compounded their declining right of bestowing crowns for subsidies to maintain a luxurious court, and to leave behind them a genealogy of wealthy heirs. The people, though exasperated by oppression, and eager for insurrection, were disunited, and not enlightened enough to bring about a lasting revolution. They revolted only to overturn their ancient laws, to change their masters, and to yield to a more arbitrary government. The monarchs, opposed by an ungovernable aristocracy, were unable to raise armies sufficient to establish their power at home, and their conquests abroad. States were aggrandized more by craft than by bravery; and their rulers became less violent, and more treacherous. The hardy crimes of the barbarous ages, gave place, by degrees, to the insidious vices of civilization. The cultivation of classical literature improved the general taste, and added to the stores of erudition; but at the same time, it enervated the boldness and originality of natural talent: and those who might have been inimitable writers in their maternal language, were satisfied to waste their powers in being the imitators of the Latins. Authors ceased to take any part in passing events, and remained distant spec-tators of them. Some detailed to their fellow-citizens the past glory, and warned them of the approaching ruin, of their country; and others repaid their patrons with flattery: for it was precisely in the fourteenth century that tyrannical governments began to teach their successors the policy of retaining men of letters in their pay to deceive the world. Such is the concise history of Italy, during the fifty-three years which elapsed from the death of Dante to the death of Petrarch.

XIII. Their endeavours to bring their country under the government of one sovereign, and to abolish the Pope's temporal power, form the only point of resemblance between these two characters. Fortune seemed to have conspired with nature, in order to separate them by an irreconcilable diversity. Dante went through a more regular course of studies, and at a time when Aristotle and Thomas Aquinas reigned alone in universities. Their stern method and maxims taught him to write only after long meditation—to keep in view "a great practical end, which is that of human life" [9]—and to pursue it steadily with a predetermined plan. Poetical ornaments seem constantly employed by Dante, only to throw a light upon his subjects; and he never allows his fancy to violate the laws which he had previously imposed upon his own genius—

L' ingegno affreno,
Perchè non corra che virtù nol guidi.—*Inferno.*
Più non mi lascia gire il fren dell' arte.—*Purg.*

I rein and curb
The powers of nature in me, lest they run
Where virtue guide not—
Mine art
With warning bridle checks me.—CARY's Transl.

The study of the classics, and the growing enthusiasm for Platonic speculations which Petrarch defended against the Aristotelians,[10] coincided with his natural inclina-

[9] Dante, Convito.
[10] This is the main object of his treatise, *De sui ipsius et multorum ignorantiâ.*

tion, and formed his mind on the works of Cicero, Seneca, and St. Augustin. He caught their desultory manner, their ornamented diction, even when handling subjects the most unpoetical; and, above all, their mixture of individual feelings with the universal principles of philosophy and religion. His pen followed the incessant restlessness of his soul: every subject allured his thoughts, and seldom were all his thoughts devoted to one alone. Thus being more eager to undertake, than persevering to complete, the great number of his unfinished manuscripts at last impressed him with the idea, that the result of industry would be little more than that of absolute idleness.[11]—Dante avows that in his youth, he was sinking beneath a long and almost unconquerable despondence; and complains of that stillness of mind which enchains the faculties without destroying them.[12] But his mind, in recovering its elasticity, never desisted until it had attained its pursuit; and no human power or interest could divert him from his meditations.[13]

XIV. The intellect of both could only act in unison with the organic and unalterable emotions of their hearts. Dante's fire was more deeply concentrated; it could burn with one passion only at a time: and if Boccaccio does not overcharge the picture, Dante, during several months after the death of Beatrice, had the feelings and appearance of a savage.[14] Petrarch was agitat-

ed at the same time by different passions: they roused, but they also counteracted, each other; and his fire was rather flashing than burning—expanding itself as it were from a soul unable to bear all its warmth, and yet anxious to attract through it the attention of every eye. Vanity made Petrarch ever eager and ever afraid of the opinion even of those individuals over whom he felt his natural superiority.— Pride was the prominent characteristic of Dante. He was pleased with his sufferings, as the means of exerting his fortitude,— and with his imperfections, as the necessary attendants of extraordinary qualities, —and with the consciousness of his internal worth, because it enabled him to look down with scorn upon other men and their opinions—

Che ti fa ciò che quivi si pispiglia?—
    Lascia dir le genti;
Sta come torre ferma che non crolla
Giammai la cima per soffiar de'venti.

                                    How
Imports it thee what thing is whisper'd here?—
    To their babblings leave
The crowd; be as a tower that firmly set,
Shakes not its top for any blast that blows.
                            CARY'S Transl.

The power of despising, which many boast, which very few really possess, and with which Dante was uncommonly gifted by nature, afforded him the highest delight of which a lofty mind is susceptible—

Lo collo poi con le braccia mi cinse,
Baciommi in volto, e disse: Alma sdegnosa!
Benedetta colei che in te s' incinse.

        Then with his arms my neck
Encircling, kiss'd my cheek and spake: O soul
Justly disdainful! blest was she in whom
Thou was conceived.
                            CARY'S Transl.

Dante's haughty demeanour towards the princes whose protection he solicited, was that of a republican by birth, an aristocrat by party, a statesman, and a warrior,

---

[11] *Quicquid ferè opusculoum mihi excidit quae tam multa fuerunt, ut usque ad hanc aetatem, me exerceant, ac fatigent: fuit enim mihi ut corpus, sic ingenium magis pollens dexteritate, quam viribus. Itaque multa mihi facilia cogitatu, quae executione difficilia praetermisi.*—Epist. ad Posterit.

[12] Dante, Vita nuova.

[13] Poggio,—Dante, Purg. cant. xvii.

[14] *He had now become, through his weeping and the affliction he felt within him, and through taking no care of his external appearance, almost a savage creature to behold—thin, bearded, and almost wholly changed from what he had used to be; so that his aspect roused compassion not merely in his friends, but indeed in every other person who saw him.* Boccaccio, Life of Dante.

who, after having lived in affluence and dignity, was proscribed in his thirty-seventh year, compelled to wander from town to town "as the man who stripping his visage of all shame, plants himself in the public way, and stretching out his hand, trembles through every vein."—"I will say no more: I know that my words are dark; but my countrymen shall help thee soon to a comment on the text, *To tremble through every vein.*" [15]—Petrarch, born in exile, and brought up, according to his own confession, in indigence,[16] and as the intended servant of a court, was year after year enriched by the great, till enabled to decline new favours, he alluded to it with the complacency inevitable to all those who, whether by chance, or industry, or merit, have escaped from penury and humiliation.

XV. Being formed to love, Petrarch courted the good-will of others, sighed for more friendship than human selfishness is willing to allow, and lowered himself in the eyes, and possibly in the affections, of the persons most devoted to him. His disappointments in this respect often embittered his soul, and extorted from him the confession, "that he feared those whom he loved." [17] His enemies knowing that, if he readily gave vent to his anger, he was still more ready to forget injuries, found fair

game for ridicule [18] in his passionate temper, and provoked him to commit himself even in his old age with apologies.[19]— Dante, on the contrary, was one of those rare individuals who are above the reach of ridicule, and whose natural dignity is enhanced, even by the blows of malignity. In his friends he inspired less commiseration than awe; in his enemies, fear and hatred —but never contempt. His wrath was inexorable; with him vengeance was not only a natural impulse but a duty: [20] and he enjoyed the certainty of that slow but everlasting revenge which "his wrath brooded over in secret silence.". . . As Petrarch without love would probably never have become a great poet—so, had it not been for injustice and persecution which kindled his indignation, Dante, perhaps, would never have persevered to complete:

> Il poema sacro,
> a cui han posto mano e cielo e terra,
> sì che mi ha fatto per molti anni macro.

> The sacred poem that hath made both heaven and earth copartners in its toil, and with lean abstinence, through many a year, faded my brow.
>
> CARY'S Transl.

---

[15] Purgat. cant. xi. towards the end.
[16] *Honestis parentibus, fortuna (ut verum fatear) ad inopiam vergente, natus sum.*—Epist. ad Post.
[17] Senil. Lib. 13. Ep. 7.

[18] *Indignantissimi animi, sed offensarum obliviosissimi—ira mihi persaepe nocuit, aliis nunquam.* —Epist. ad Post.
[19] Agostini, Scritt. Venez. vol. 1. p. 5.
[20] *Che bell' onor s' acquista in far vendetta.* Dante, Convito.—See also, Inferno, cant. xxix. vers. 31-36.

Goethe

A Discussion of Dante

. . . The conversation turned once more on the bust of Dante, which stood before us, and on his life and works. The obscurity of this author was especially mentioned—how his own countrymen had never understood him, so that it would be impossible for a foreigner to penetrate such darkness. "To you," said Goethe, turning towards me with a friendly air, "the study of this poet is absolutely forbidden by your father confessor."

Goethe also remarked that the difficult rhyme is, in a great measure, the cause of his obscurity. For the rest, he spoke of Dante with extreme reverence; and I observed that he was not satisfied with the word *talent*, but called him a *nature*, as if thus wishing to express something more comprehensive, more full of prescience, of deeper insight, and wider scope.

Friday, Dec. 3, 1824.

From *Conversations of Goethe with Eckermann*, translated by J. Oxenford, reprinted in Everyman's Library; used by permission of E. P. Dutton & Co., Inc.

John Ruskin

Dante's Landscape

MILTON's effort, in all that he tells us of his Inferno, is to make it indefinite; Dante's, to make it *definite*. Both, indeed, describe it as entered through gates; but, within the gate, all is wild and fenceless with Milton, having indeed its four rivers,—the last vestige of the mediaeval tradition,—but rivers which flow through a waste of mountain and moorland, and by "many a frozen, many a fiery Alp." But Dante's Inferno is accurately separated into circles drawn with well-pointed compasses; mapped and properly surveyed in every direction, trenched in a thoroughly good style of engineering from depth to depth, and divided in the "*accurate* middle" (dritto mezzo) of its deepest abyss, into a concentric series of ten moats and embankments, like those about a castle, with bridges from each embankment to the next; precisely in the manner of those bridges over Hiddekel and Euphrates, which Mr. Macaulay thinks so innocently designed, apparently not aware that he is also laughing at Dante. These larger fosses are of rock, and the bridges also; but as he goes farther into detail, Dante tells us of various minor fosses and embankments, in which he anxiously points out to us not only the formality, but the neatness and perfectness, of the stonework. For instance, in describing the river Phlegethon, he tells us that it was "paved with stone at the bottom, and at the sides, and *over the edges of the sides*," just as the water is at the baths of Bulicame; and for fear we should think this embankment at all *larger* than it really was, Dante adds, carefully, that it was made just like the embankments of Ghent or Bruges against the sea, or those in Lombardy which bank the Brenta, only "not so high, nor so wide," as any of these. And besides the trenches, we have two well-built castles; one, like Ecbatana, with seven circuits of wall (and surrounded by a fair stream), wherein the great poets and sages of antiquity live; and another, a great fortified city with walls of iron, red-hot, and a deep fosse round it, and full of "grave citizens,"—the city of Dis.

§ 30. Now, whether this be in what we moderns call "good taste," or not, I do not mean just now to inquire—Dante having nothing to do with taste, but with the facts of what he had seen; only, so far as the imaginative faculty of the two poets is concerned, note that Milton's vagueness is not the sign of imagination, but of its absence, so far as it is significative in the matter. For it does not follow, because Milton did not map out his Inferno as Dante did, that he *could* not have done so if he had chosen; only, it was the easier and less imaginative process to leave it vague than to define it. Imagination is always the seeing and asserting faculty; that which obscures or conceals may be judgment, or feeling, but not invention. The invention, whether good or bad, is in the accurate engineering, not in the fog and uncertainty.

§ 31. When we pass with Dante from the Inferno to Purgatory, we have indeed more light and air, but no more liberty; being now confined on various ledges cut into a mountain side, with a precipice on one hand and a vertical wall on the other; and,

From *Modern Painters*, vol. III, "Of Mediaeval Landscape," 1856.

lest here also we should make any mistake about magnitudes, we are told that the ledges were eighteen feet wide,[1] and that the ascent from one to the other was by steps, made like those which go up from Florence to the church of San Miniato.[2]

Lastly, though in the Paradise there is perfect freedom and infinity of space, though for trenches we have planets, and for cornices constellations, yet there is more cadence, procession, and order among the redeemed souls than any others; they fly, so as to describe letters and sentences in the air, and rest in circles, like rainbows, or determinate figures, as of a cross and an eagle; in which certain of the more glorified natures are so arranged as to form the eye of the bird, while those most highly blessed are arranged with their white crowds in leaflets, so as to form the image of a white rose in the midst of heaven.

§ 32. Thus, throughout the poem, I conceive that the first striking character of its scenery is intense definition; precisely the reflection of that definiteness which we have already traced in pictorial art. But the second point which seems noteworthy is, that the flat ground and embanked trenches are reserved for the Inferno; and that the entire territory of the Purgatory is a mountain, thus marking the sense of that purifying and perfecting influence in mountains which we saw the mediaeval mind was so ready to suggest. The same general idea is indicated at the very commencement of the poem, in which Dante is overwhelmed by fear and sorrow in passing through a dark forest, but revives on seeing the sun touch the top of a hill, afterwards called by Virgil "the pleasant mount—the cause and source of all delight."

§ 33. While, however, we find this greater honour paid to mountains, I think we may perceive a much greater dread and dislike of woods. We saw that Homer seemed to attach a pleasant idea, for the most part,

[1] "Three times the length of the human body."—Purg. x. 24.
[2] Purg. xii. 102.

to forests; regarding them as sources of wealth and places of shelter; and we find constantly an idea of sacredness attached to them, as being haunted especially by the gods; so that even the wood which surrounds the house of Circe is spoken of as a sacred thicket, or rather, as a sacred glade, or labyrinth of glades (of the particular word used I shall have more to say presently); and so the wood is sought as a kindly shelter by Ulysses, in spite of its wild beasts; and evidently regarded with great affection by Sophocles, for, in a passage which is always regarded by readers of Greek tragedy with peculiar pleasure, the aged and blind Oedipus, brought to rest in "the sweetest resting-place" in all the neighbourhood of Athens, has the spot described to him as haunted perpetually by nightingales, which sing "in the green glades and in the dark ivy, and in the thousand-fruited sunless, and windless thickets of the god" (Bacchus); the idea of the complete shelter from wind and sun being here, as with Ulysses, the uppermost one. After this come the usual staples of landscape,—narcissus, crocus, plenty of rain, olive trees; and last, and the greatest boast of all,—"it is a good country for horses, and conveniently by the sea"; but the prominence and pleasantness of the thick wood in the thoughts of the writer are very notable; whereas to Dante the idea of a forest is exceedingly repulsive, so that, as just noticed, in the opening of his poem, he cannot express a general despair about life more strongly than by saying he was lost in a wood so savage and terrible, that "even to think or speak of it is distress,—it was so bitter,—it was something next door to death"; and one of the saddest scenes in all the Inferno is in a forest, of which the trees are haunted by lost souls; while (with only one exception), whenever the country is to be beautiful, we find ourselves coming out into open air and open meadows.

It is quite true that this is partly a characteristic, not merely of Dante, or of mediaeval writers, but of *southern* writers; for the simple reason that the forest, being with them higher upon the hills, and more out of the way than in the north, was generally a type of lonely and savage places; while in England, the "greenwood," coming up to the very walls of the towns, it was possible to be "merry in the good greenwood," in a sense which an Italian could not have understood. Hence Chaucer, Spenser, and Shakspere send their favourites perpetually to the woods for pleasure or meditation; and trust their tender Canace, or Rosalind, or Helena, or Silvia, or Belphoebe, where Dante would have sent no one but a condemned spirit. Nevertheless, there is always traceable in the mediaeval mind a dread of thick foliage, which was not present to that of a Greek; so that, even in the north, we have our sorrowful "children in the wood," and black huntsmen of the Hartz forests, and such other wood terrors; the principal reason for the difference being that a Greek, being by no means given to travelling, regarded his woods as so much valuable property; and if he ever went into them for pleasure, expected to meet one or two gods in the course of his walk, but no banditti; while a mediaeval, much more of a solitary traveller, and expecting to meet with no gods in the thickets, but only with thieves, or a hostile ambush, or a bear, besides a great deal of troublesome ground for his horse, and a very serious chance, next to a certainty, of losing his way, naturally kept in the open ground as long as he could, and regarded the forests, in general, with anything but an eye of favour.

§ 34. These, I think, are the principal points which must strike us, when we first broadly think of the poem as compared with classical work. Let us now go a little more into detail.

As Homer gave us an ideal landscape, which even a god might have been pleased to behold, so Dante gives us, fortunately, an ideal landscape, which is specially intended for the terrestrial paradise. And it will doubtless be with some surprise, after our reflections above on the general tone of Dante's feelings, that we find ourselves here first entering a *forest*, and that even a *thick* forest. But there is a peculiar meaning in this. With any other poet than Dante, it might have been regarded as a wanton inconsistency. Not so with him: by glancing back to the two lines which explain the nature of Paradise, we shall see what he means by it. Virgil tells him, as he enters it, "Henceforward, take thine own pleasure for guide; thou art beyond the steep ways, and beyond all Art";—meaning, that the perfectly purified and noble human creature, having no pleasure but in right, is past all effort, and past all *rule*. Art has no existence for such a being. Hence, the first aim of Dante, in his landscape imagery, is to show evidence of this perfect liberty, and of the purity and sinlessness of the new nature, converting pathless ways into happy ones. So that all those fences and formalisms which had been needed for him in imperfection, are removed in this paradise; and even the pathlessness of the wood, the most dreadful thing possible to him in his days of sin and shortcoming, is now a joy to him in his days of purity. And as the fencelessness and thicket of sin led to the fettered and fearful order of eternal punishment, so the fencelessness and thicket of the free virtue lead to the loving and constellated order of eternal happiness.

§ 35. This forest, then, is very like that of Colonos in several respects—in its peace and sweetness, and number of birds; it differs from it only in letting a light breeze through it, being therefore somewhat thinner than the Greek wood; the tender lines which tell of the voices of the birds mingling with the wind, and of the leaves all turning one way before it, have been more or less copied by every poet since Dante's time. They are, so far as I know, the sweetest passage of wood description which exists in literature.

Before, however, Dante has gone far in

this wood,—that is to say, only so far as to have lost sight of the place where he entered it, or rather, I suppose, of the light under the boughs of the outside trees, and it must have been a very thin wood indeed if he did not do this in some quarter of a mile's walk,—he comes to a little river, three paces over, which bends the blades of grass to the left, with a meadow on the other side of it; and in this meadow

> "A lady, graced with solitude, who went
>   Singing, and setting flower by flower apart,
> By which the path she walked on was besprent.
> 'Ah, lady beautiful, that basking art
>   In beams of love, if I may trust thy face,
>   Which useth to bear witness of the heart,
> Let liking come on thee,' said I, 'to trace
>   Thy path a little closer to the shore,
>   Where I may reap the hearing of thy lays.
> Thou mindest me, how Proserpine of yore
>   Appeared in such a place, what time her mother
> Lost her, and she the spring, for evermore.'
> As, pointing downwards and to one another
>   Her feet, a lady bendeth in the dance,
>   And barely setteth one before the other,
> Thus, on the scarlet and the saffron glance
>   Of flowers, with motion maidenlike she bent
> (Her modest eyelids drooping and askance);
> And there she gave my wishes their content,
>   Approaching, so that her sweet melodies
> Arrived upon mine ear with what they meant.
> When first she came amongst the blades, that rise,
>   Already wetted, from the goodly river,
> She graced me by the lifting of her eyes."
> —CAYLEY.

§ 36. I have given this passage at length, because, for our purposes, it is by much the most important, not only in Dante, but in the whole circle of poetry. This lady, observe, stands on the opposite side of the little stream, which, presently, she explains to Dante is Lethe, having power to cause forgetfulness of all evil, and she stands just among the bent blades of grass at its edge. She is first seen gathering flower from flower, then "passing continually the multitudinous flowers through her hands," smiling at the same time so brightly, that her

first address to Dante is to prevent him from wondering at her, saying, "if he will remember the verse of the ninety-second Psalm, beginning 'Delectasti,' he will know why she is so happy."

And turning to the verse of this Psalm we find it written, "Thou, Lord, hast made me glad *through Thy works*. I will triumph *in the works of Thy hands*"; or, in the very words in which Dante would read it,—

> "Quia delectasti me, Domine, in factura tua,
> Et in operibus manuum Tuarum exultabo."

§ 37. Now we could not for an instant have had any difficulty in understanding this, but that, some way farther on in the poem, this lady is called Matilda, and is with reason supposed by the commentators to be the great Countess Matilda of the eleventh century; notable equally for her ceaseless activity, her brilliant political genius, her perfect piety, and her deep reverence for the see of Rome. This Countess Matilda is therefore Dante's guide in the terrestrial paradise, as Beatrice is afterward in the celestial; each of them having a spiritual and symbolic character in their glorified state, yet retaining their definite personality.

The question is, then, what is the symbolic character of the Countess Matilda, as the guiding spirit of the terrestrial paradise? Before Dante had entered this paradise he had rested on a step of shelving rock, and as he watched the stars he slept, and dreamed, and thus tells us what he saw:—

> "A lady, young and beautiful, I dreamed,
>   Was passing o'er a lea; and, as she came,
>   Methought I saw her ever and anon
> Bending to cull the flowers; and thus she sang:
> 'Know ye, whoever of my name would ask,
>   That I am Leah; for my brow to weave
> A garland, these fair hands unwearied ply;
>   To please me at the crystal mirror, here
> I deck me. But my sister Rachel, she
>   Before her glass abides the livelong day,
> Her radiant eyes beholding, charmed no less
>   Than I with this delightful task. Her joy
> In contemplation, as in labour mine.'"

This vision of Rachel and Leah has been always, and with unquestionable truth, received as a type of the Active and Contemplative life, and as an introduction to the two divisions of the paradise which Dante is about to enter. Therefore the unwearied spirit of the Countess Matilda is understood to represent the Active life, which forms the felicity of Earth; and the spirit of Beatrice the Contemplative life, which forms the felicity of Heaven. This interpretation appears at first straightforward and certain; but it has missed count of exactly the most important fact in the two passages which we have to explain. Observe: Leah gathers the flowers to decorate *herself*, and delights in *Her Own* Labour. Rachel sits silent, contemplating herself, and the delights of *Her Own* Image. These are the types of the Unglorified Active and Contemplative powers of Man. But Beatrice and Matilda are the same powers, Glorified. And how are they Glorified? Leah took delight in her own labour; but Matilda—"in operibus *manuum Tuarum*"—in God's labour: Rachel in the sight of her own face; Beatrice in the sight of *God's face*.

§ 38. And thus, when afterwards Dante sees Beatrice on her throne, and prays her that, when he himself shall die, she would receive him with kindness, Beatrice merely looks down for an instant, and answers with a single smile, then "towards the eternal fountain turns."

Therefore it is evident that Dante distinguishes in both cases, not between earth and heaven, but between perfect and imperfect happiness, whether in earth or heaven. The active life which has only the service of man for its end, and therefore gathers flowers, with Leah, for its own decoration, is indeed happy, but not perfectly so; it has only the happiness of the dream, belonging essentially to the dream of human life, and passing away with it. But the active life which labours for the more and more discovery of God's work, is perfectly happy, and is the life of the terrestrial paradise, being a true foretaste of heaven, and be-

ginning in earth, as heaven's vestibule. So also the contemplative life which is concerned with human feeling and thought and beauty—the life which is in earthly poetry and imagery of noble earthly emotion—is happy, but it is the happiness of the dream; the contemplative life which has God's person and love in Christ for its object, has the happiness of eternity. But because this higher happiness is also begun here on earth, Beatrice descends to earth; and when revealed to Dante first, he sees the image of the twofold personality of Christ reflected in her *eyes;* as the flowers, which are, to the mediaeval heart, the chief work of God, are for ever passing through Matilda's *hands*.

§ 39. Now, therefore, we see that Dante, as the great prophetic exponent of the heart of the Middle Ages, has, by the lips of the spirit of Matilda, declared the mediaeval faith,—that all perfect active life was "the expression of man's delight *in God's work*"; and that all their political and warlike energy, as fully shown in the mortal life of Matilda, was yet inferior and impure,—the energy of the dream,—compared with that which on the opposite bank of Lethe stood "choosing flower from flower." And what joy and peace there were in this work is marked by Matilda's being the person who draws Dante through the stream of Lethe, so as to make him forget all sin, and all sorrow: throwing her arms round him, she plunges his head under the waves of it; then draws him through, crying to him, *"hold me, hold me"* (tiemmi, tiemmi), and so presents him, thus bathed, free from all painful memory, at the feet of the spirit of the more heavenly contemplation.

§ 40. The reader will, I think, now see, with sufficient distinctness, why I called this passage the most important, for our present purposes, in the whole circle of poetry. For it contains the first great confession of the discovery by the human race (I mean as a matter of experience, not of revelation), that their happiness was not in themselves, and that their labour was not to have their own service as its chief end. It embodies in a few syllables the *sealing* difference between the Greek and the mediaeval, in that the former sought the flower and herb for his own uses, the latter for God's honour; the former, primarily and on principle, contemplated his own beauty and the workings of his own mind, and the latter, primarily and on principle, contemplated Christ's beauty and the workings of the mind of Christ.

§ 41. I will not at present follow up this subject any farther; it being enough that we have thus got to the root of it, and have a great declaration of the central mediaeval purpose, whereto we may return for solution of all future questions. I would only, therefore, desire the reader now to compare the Stones of Venice, vol. i. chap. xx. §§ 15, 16; the Seven Lamps of Architecture, chap. iv. § 3; and the second volume of this work, chap. II. §§ 9, 10. and chap. III. § 10; that he may, in these several places, observe how gradually our conclusions are knitting themselves together as we are able to determine more and more of the successive questions that come before us: and, finally, to compare the two interesting passages in Wordsworth, which, without any memory of Dante, nevertheless, as if by some special ordaining, describe in matters of modern life exactly the soothing or felicitous powers of the two active spirits of Dante—Leah and Matilda, Excursion, book v. line 608. to 625., and book vi. line 102. to 214.

§ 42. Having thus received from Dante this great lesson, as to the spirit in which mediaeval landscape is to be understood, what else we have to note respecting it, as seen in his poem, will be comparatively straightforward and easy. And first, we have to observe the place occupied in his mind by *colour*. It has already been shown, in the Stones of Venice, vol. ii. chap. v. §§ 30–34., that colour is the most *sacred* element of all visible things. Hence, as the mediaeval mind contemplated them first

for their sacredness, we should, beforehand, expect that the first thing it would seize would be the colour; and that we should find its expressions and renderings of colour infinitely more loving and accurate than among the Greeks.

§ 43. Accordingly, the Greek sense of colour seems to have been so comparatively dim and uncertain, that it is almost impossible to ascertain what the real idea was which they attached to any word alluding to hue: and above all, colour, though pleasant to their eyes, as to those of all human beings, seems never to have been impressive to their feelings. They liked purple, on the whole, the best; but there was no sense of cheerfulness or pleasantness in one colour, and gloom in another, such as the mediaevals had.

For instance, when Achilles goes, in great anger and sorrow, to complain to Thetis of the scorn done him by Agamemnon, the sea appears to him "wine-coloured." One might think this meant that the sea looked dark and reddish-purple to him, in a kind of sympathy with his anger. But we turn to the passage of Sophocles, which has been above quoted,—a passage peculiarly intended to express peace and rest,—and we find that the birds sing among "wine-coloured" ivy. The uncertainty of conception of the hue itself, and entire absence of expressive character in the word, could hardly be more clearly manifested.

§ 44. Again: I said the Greek liked purple, as a general source of enjoyment, better than any other colour. So he did; and so all healthy persons who have eye for colour, and are unprejudiced about it, do; and will to the end of time, for a reason presently to be noted. But so far was this instinctive preference for purple from giving, in the Greek mind, any consistently cheerful or sacred association to the colour, that Homer constantly calls death "purple death."

§ 45. Again: in the passage of Sophocles, so often spoken of, I said there was some difficulty respecting a word often translated "thickets." I believe, myself, it means glades; literally, "going places" in the woods,—that is to say, places where, either naturally or by force, the trees separate, so as to give some accessible avenue. Now, Sophocles tells us the birds sang in these "*green* going places"; and we take up the expression gratefully, thinking the old Greek perceived and enjoyed, as we do, the sweet fall of the eminently *green* light through the leaves when they are a little thinner than in the heart of the wood. But we turn to the tragedy of Ajax, and are much shaken in our conclusion about the meaning of the word, when we are told that the body of Ajax is to lie unburied, and be eaten by sea-birds on the "*green* sand." The formation, geologically distinguished by that title, was certainly not known to Sophocles; and the only conclusion which, it seems to me, we can come to under the circumstances,—assuming Ariel's [3] authority as to the colour of pretty sand, and the ancient mariner's (or, rather, his hearer's [4]) as to the colour of ugly sand, to be conclusive,—is that Sophocles really did not know green from yellow or brown.

§ 46. Now, without going out of the terrestrial paradise, in which Dante last left us, we shall be able at once to compare with this Greek incertitude the precision of the mediaeval eye for colour. Some three arrowflights farther up into the wood we come to a tall tree, which is at first barren, but, after some little time, visibly opens into flowers, of a colour "less than that of roses, but more than that of violets."

It certainly would not be possible, in words, to come nearer to the *definition* of the exact hue which Dante meant—that of the apple-blossom. Had he employed any simple colour-phrase, as a "pale pink," or "violet-pink," or any other such combined expression, he still could not have completely got at the delicacy of the hue; he might perhaps have indicated its kind, but not its tenderness; but by taking the rose-leaf as the type of the delicate red, and then enfeebling this with the violet grey, he gets, as closely as language can carry him, to the complete rendering of the vision, though it is evidently felt by him to be in its perfect beauty ineffable; and rightly so felt, for of all lovely things which grace the spring time in our fair temperate zone, I am not sure but this blossoming of the apple-tree is the fairest. At all events, I find it associated in my mind with four other kinds of colour, certainly principal among the gifts of the northern earth, namely:

1st. Bell gentians growing close together, mixed with lilies of the valley, on the Jura pastures.
2d. Alpine roses with dew upon them, under low rays of morning sunshine, touching the tops of the flowers.
3d. Bell heather in mass, in full light, at sunset.
4th. White narcissus (red-centred) in mass, on the Vevay pastures, in sunshine, after rain.

And I know not where in the group to place the wreaths of apple-blossoms in the Vevay orchards, with the far-off blue of the lake of Geneva seen between the flowers.

A Greek, however, would have regarded this blossom simply with the eyes of a Devonshire farmer, as bearing on the probable price of cider, and would have called it red, cerulean, purple, white, hyacinthine, or generally "aglaos," agreeable, as happened to suit his verse.

§ 47. Again: we have seen how fond the Greek was of composing his paradises of rather damp grass; but that in this fondness for grass there was always an undercurrent of consideration for his horses; and the characters in it which pleased him most were its depth and freshness; not its colour. Now, if we remember carefully the general expressions, respecting grass, used

---

[3] "Come unto these *yellow* sands."
[4] "And thou art long, and lank, and *brown,*
  As is the ribbed sea sand."

in modern literature, I think nearly the commonest that occurs to us will be that of "enamelled" turf or sward. This phrase is usually employed by our pseudo-poets, like all their other phrases, without knowing what it means, because it has been used by other writers before them, and because they do not know what else to say of grass. If we were to ask them what enamel was, they could not tell us; and if we asked why grass was like enamel, they could not tell us. The expression *has* a meaning, however, and one peculiarly characteristic of mediaeval and modern temper.

§ 48. The first instance I know of its right use, though very probably it had been so employed before, is in Dante. The righteous spirits of the pre-Christian ages are seen by him, though in the Inferno, yet in a place open, luminous, and high, walking upon the "green enamel."

I am very sure that Dante did not use this phrase as we use it. He knew well what enamel was; and his readers, in order to understand him thoroughly, must remember what it is,—a vitreous paste, dissolved in water, mixed with metallic oxides, to give it the opacity and the colour required, spread in a moist state on metal, and afterwards hardened by fire, so as never to change. And Dante means, in using this metaphor of the grass of the Inferno, to mark that it is laid as a tempering and cooling substance over the dark, metallic, gloomy ground; but yet so hardened by the fire, that it is not any more fresh or living grass, but a smooth, silent, lifeless bed of eternal green. And we know how *hard* Dante's idea of it was; because afterwards, in what is perhaps the most awful passage of the whole Inferno, when the three furies rise at the top of the burning tower, and catching sight of Dante, and not being able to get at him, shriek wildly for the Gorgon to come up too, that they may turn him into stone,—the word *stone* is not hard enough for them. Stone might crumble away after it was made, or something with life might grow upon it; no, it

shall not be stone; they will make enamel of him; nothing can grow out of that; it is dead for ever.[5]

"Venga Medusa, si lo farem di *Smalto*."

§49. Now, almost in the opening of the Purgatory, as there at the entrance of the Inferno, we find a company of great ones resting in a grassy place. But the idea of the grass is now very different. The word now used is not "enamel," but "herb," and instead of being merely green, it is covered with flowers of many colours. With the usual mediaeval accuracy, Dante insists on telling us precisely what these colours were, and how bright; which he does by naming the actual pigments used in illumination,—"Gold, and fine silver, and cochineal, and white lead, and Indian wood, serene and lucid, and fresh emerald, just broken, would have been excelled, as less is by greater, by the flowers and grass of the place." It is evident that the "emerald" here means the emerald green of the illuminators; for a fresh emerald is no brighter than one which is not fresh, and Dante was not one to throw away his words thus. Observe, then, we have here the idea of the growth, life, and variegation of the "green herb," as opposed to the *smalto* of the Inferno; but the colours of the variegation are illustrated and defined by the reference to actual pigments; and, observe, because the other colours are rather bright, the blue ground (Indian wood, indigo?) is sober; lucid, but serene; and presently two angels enter, who are dressed in green drapery, but of a paler green than the grass, which Dante marks, by telling us that it was "the green of leaves just budded."

§ 50. In all this, I wish the reader to observe two things: first, the general carefulness of the poet in defining colour, distinguishing it precisely as a painter would (opposed to the Greek carelessness about it); and, secondly, his regarding the grass

[5] Compare parallel passage, making Dante hard or changeless in good, Purg. viii. 114.

for its greenness and variegation, rather than, as a Greek would have done, for its depth and freshness. This greenness or brightness, and variegation, are taken up by later and modern poets, as the things intended to be chiefly expressed by the word "enamelled"; and, gradually, the term is taken to indicate any kind of bright and interchangeable colouring; there being always this much of propriety about it, when used of greensward, that such sward is indeed, like enamel, a coat of bright colour on a comparatively dark ground; and is thus a sort of natural jewellery and painter's work, different from loose and large vegetation. The word is often awkwardly and falsely used, by the later poets, of all kinds of growth and colour; as by Milton of the flowers of Paradise showing themselves over its wall; but it retains, nevertheless, through all its jaded inanity, some half-unconscious vestige of the old sense, even to the present day.

Giosuè Carducci

Lecture on Dante

. . . Barred from returning to Florence by the outrageous terms of pardon that had been proposed to him, Dante felt the last remnants of his faith in the actual world shattered. But his grief generated a higher objective: he set his gaze now where the human mind had never looked before. Out of the silences of the barbarian age Virgil came towards him through the "savage wood," pointing him on towards the mount of virtue and glory; Beatrice, whom he had always loved in the solitude of his loftiest thought, beckoned him from heaven. Death and eternity attracted him. The infinite opened out before his sublime imagination, and upon it he saw projected past, present, and future under the sway of religion, history, and poetry. Dante sought his country now in the other world. He fixed his eyes on the highest heaven and located his ideal there where neither the outrages of the Guelphs nor the venom of the cloistered could reach.

Between two deaths—that of Henry VII and that of Beatrice [1]—the idea of the poem of death came to maturity; by the time the poet himself died, it was fully realized. All that he had written, thought, or done so far came to focus in the Comedy, which is the figurative embodiment of the Vita Nuova's final vision, the actualization of the moral and allegorical system of the Convivio, the glorification of De Vulgari Eloquentia, the consecration of the Monarchia. In the dolce stil nuovo rhymes Dante had addressed himself to true lovers; in the Convivio to the aristocrats of Italy; in the Latin treatises to clerics and doctors. In the Comedy the poet sings to the whole people—all peoples. In the rhymes he was a Florentine—first among mediaeval lyricists; in the treatises he was an Italian—first lay philosopher of the Middle Ages; in the Comedy, without ceasing to be the foremost poet of the period, he is more largely the poet par excellence of the Latin world and of Christianity; he is furthermore the poet, in the sovereign sense of the word, of all times.

The protagonists of Dante's epic divine world are three: Dante, Virgil, and Beatrice. Its action is the present world—active, moral, intellective—reflected and projected with boundless imaginative power in the after-life scene where thought has no limitations other than those imposed by the mind of the creator-poet.

Beatrice is a product of the Vita Nuova as well as of chivalric and mystic poetry; but in the vision on the summit of Purgatory the cult of woman becomes apotheosis, and the transfigured Beatrice is the supreme representation of mediaeval civility. Virgil emerges from the classical teachings of the Convivio: he is no longer the wizard the Middle Ages had made of him, but neither is he merely the poet of the schoolmen: he has become a representation of the civilization of antiquity. Standing between antiquity and the Middle Ages—between Virgil and Beatrice—Dante is man, the human creature going his way, weighted with all his passions, loving and hating, erring and falling, repenting and rising, and—once purged and reborn—worthy of mounting into the full perfection of being.

[1] Beatrice Portinari.

From G. Carducci, *Discorsi Letterari e Storici*, Bologna, Zanichelli, 1889. Translated and excerpted by the editor.

Thus the *Comedy* is, as the poet said, a doctrinal work; it actualizes the moral philosophy of the *Convivio*, and especially the affirmation that the human soul tends towards perfection and felicity and moves towards them by two avenues and in two ways. Its subject is man as, through the gift of free will, he is subject to rewarding and punishing justice; its goal is to remove those living in this world from a state of misery and to direct them towards temporal perfection and felicity through the exercise of the philosophic virtues, and towards eternal perfection and beatitude through the exercise of the theological virtues. Given its author's faith and times, no such teaching could have been embodied in poetry unless in terms harmonious with Christian belief. Hence the vision of the damned, the penitent, and the blessed souls in the other world. Under the cover of which allegory the moral meaning is clearly demonstrative of the three states of souls in the *present* world: namely, sin, conversion, and virtue. With respect to the soul's tendency towards perfection by two avenues, temporal and eternal, the allegory has two senses: the tropological, whereby it sets forth the moral rule of human life; and the anagogical, whereby it draws from the poetic fiction a reference to the eternal life according to theology.

Thus at the earthly base of the poem, in the Dark Wood, it is Virgil—symbol of reason, philosophy, and empire—who first comes forward to lead Dante, the man, to his vision of temporal perfection in the Terrestrial Paradise. It is Beatrice, symbol of faith, of theology, of the Church, who descends from heaven to raise Dante into the presence of eternal perfection and beatitude in the Empyrean.

The *Comedy*, then, actualizes a moral conception under the pious form of the vision, using allegory with hortatory purpose. In so far as we find the organic conception of the work embodied in the vision, the poetry is epic and lyric. In so far as we find it in actions of human beings, souls, personified symbols, the poetry is dramatic. Where the purpose is hortatory, the poetry is didactic. In point of fact, the *Comedy* embodies poetry of every possible nuance, demonstrating a universality no other age or individual has achieved.

The architecture of the three realms of death, too, is informed by a mediaeval conception, but with extraordinary liberty and daring of imagination. Inferno does not follow the patristic or popular version. Hell, with its circles and sub-circles illustrating the divisions of sin according to Christian doctrine modified by Aristotle's *Ethics*, plunges canyon-like to the center of the earth. Its origin and nature are set forth with such dynamic moral sublimity and inventiveness that the reader is filled with terror and wonder. Dante imagines Lucifer as having plunged halfway through the earth in his fall from heaven; the displaced earth, in order to flee him, has heaped itself up in the southern hemisphere, forming the island and the mount of Purgatory. The monster is planted exactly in the center of the earth with his head emerging into the last round of Inferno (the icy quarters of the traitors), facing Jerusalem where the sinless man, Jesus, lived and died; he thrusts his feet towards the other hemisphere—towards the mount where the first man, Adam, sinned. Thus Lucifer, or evil itself, stands between the two poles of sin and redemption, and with his fall originates Purgatory, which is the means of redemption.

The mountain of Purgatory, springing straight towards the sky from the hemisphere of waters, is entirely of Dante's invention, except as it may reflect old historic or poetic legends of unknown distant lands, and more recent hints, from the Italian explorers, of new worlds waiting to be discovered. The fair mountain, ordered and compartmented according to the Platonic doctrine that identifies all error with a disordering of love, sends up to God from its circular terraces the voices of souls in prayer and song; and, when one of these souls frees itself in sudden capacity to rise upward, the holy mountain trembles with love, while a praise of God rises from thousands of spirit-voices throughout infinite spaces of sea and sky. At the top, the divine forest of the Earthly Paradise blooms and murmurs; and here, at the outmost boundaries of our planet, the traveler is accorded a miraculous vision of Empire and Church.

Paradise is made up of the nine heavens of the Ptolemaic astronomy, arranged in hierarchy according to the writings of Dionysius the Areopagite.[2] These nine realms of intellectual tranquillity counterbalance the nine circles of sin—which is to say, of spiritual turbulence—in Inferno and Purgatory; they symbolize the seven liberal arts of the trivium and the quadrivium, and natural and moral wisdom. Spherical in form, they contain and embrace one another. Our planet, being their center, is wrapped in their continual rotation, which spreads, widens, and increases, more and more, outwards to the ninth—the *Primo Mobile*—which whirls with immeasurable rapidity. The *Primo Mobile* is a frontier between the human and the divine. Beneath it, in the eighth or Starry Heaven, Dante records the outburst of the Apostle Peter's wrath against the wickedness of his successors, as well as Beatrice's rebuke to the preachers. Above it, in the Empyrean, within the triumph of Paradise, we see the glittering throne of the lofty and ill-fated emperor Henry VII. Beatrice points it out to the poet, utters a final judgment on the pontiff who failed the emperor, then takes her own place close to God. And the human scene closes. In contrast to the vertiginous speed of the *Primo Mobile*, there is in the Empyrean motionless tranquillity. This is the heaven of theology, of God's immediate presence surrounded by the nine angelic orders in their triple grouping.

[2] *The Celestial Hierarchy*, formerly attributed to Dionysius, is now acknowledged to have been the work of anonymous neoplatonists of the fifth or sixth century.—Ed.

Each order is engaged in moving its corresponding heaven by means of its own characteristic virtue; each virtue is love, raying forth from God, penetrating the whole universe with light and summoning it to life. Thus, the good. Evil, relegated to earth's center in the form of Lucifer, is in every part equally remote from that life, light, and love which he neither sees, feels, nor shares.

Such is Dante's sacred poem. And while it outstrips by far his other works and those of his contemporaries, it embodies certain attributes to which our own age cannot respond. Even as early as in the *Vita Nuova*, Beatrice's person and actions were governed by the number nine; whence, since three is the root of nine, Beatrice was said to be a miracle stemming from the wondrous Trinity. Three and nine govern the whole vision and poetry of the *Comedy*. The Trinity, surrounded by the nine orders of the three angelic hierarchies, controls the three realms; each of these, broken into nine subdivisions, is sung in thirty-three cantos formed of three-line stanzas; the sum of the cantos (leaving aside the first of the *Inferno*, which is a general prologue) is ninety-nine.—And yet, all this *cabala* of numbers served as a curb upon the work of art and led to the proportioned, harmonious, almost mathematical formal execution of the immense epic.

Essentially it is a *popular* work. The poet showed his allegiance to the genius of the people in the very selection of his meter—derived from one of the forms of Italian narrative poetry heard throughout the streets of Italy: namely, the *sirventese*. And it was with the purpose of reaching the audience he most cared for that he renounced the *illustre*, or "exalted" Italian style, and adopted the style he himself had termed "comic" (by implication, lowly), which in fact represents the gamut of truth. The basic fiction of the *Comedy* is altogether popular. The future life, of which this present is the merest false adumbration, and for which it may at most be a pious preparation, had filled the best thought of mediaeval men—and, indeed, of the entire Christian world—for twelve centuries. Dante was the voice of those centuries which themselves had been mute with terror and ignorance in the presence of the visionary hallucinations that came to them out of their various Hellenic, Italic, Semitic, druidic, Nordic memories and origins. In his great role he was the supreme representative of the Latin peoples, who before now had originated no poetry properly their own—yet who had, during the long winter of the barbarian age, ripened the germ of their own spring in the rich seed-ground of the people.

It was out of the mutual tempering of bloods and races, source of the new nobility of the Italian people, that Dante sprang up to achieve his insight into the complex Christian world. The lines of his face reveal the Etruscan type—as one finds it in obstinate persistence throughout Tuscany, blending with the Roman and dominating it. He boasted of Roman blood. The fact that his family considered itself to be of the old Florentine stock, and that it bore no titles of feudal nobility and was without foreign names until a late date—all this makes it credible that they had descended in direct line from the original settlers who had preserved their stock in a city and a region removed from the path of the Germanic invasions. But German blood did, by chance, flow in Dante's veins. It came to him through Cacciaguida's [3] wife—a native of the Po Valley and a daughter of the noble old Ferrarese Aldighieri family, into which a strain of Longobard blood had infused new vigor. It was this lady who gave her grandchildren their Germanic surname. And thus it would seem that the Allighieri poet brought to his Christian visionary poem something of the priestly Etruscan bent for otherworld mys-

[3] For Cacciaguida see Par. XV, 13 ff.

teries; an uprightness and tenacity inherited from the great civilizing race of the Romans, whose poetry was the law; and the bold freshness and freedom of the young German warrior people.

Hence the deep sincerity of his vision, the intensity and incandescence of the work, the sureness of approach to essentials in the fiction, the inward tone of the impassioned imagination, the musical sense informing the creative thought. In this poetry there is the ingenuousness of popular song . . . and there is the tension of the prophetic hymn. . . . There is a robust, graceful, lively variety of colors, sounds, and views—reminiscent of the hillscapes of Tuscany; there is a terrible and scabrous grotesque element, emerging against sooty darkness, as in the feverish air of the cork groves of the old Maremme; there is splendor diffused throughout the serene vastness of the poem, as pensive and cordial as a spring day on the Tyrrhenian Sea; there is a pure response of spiritual joy in the lucidity of an idea—immaculate, clear, and tranquil as a summer day in the Alps.

Such is the emergence of Dante in the final twilight of the Middle Ages and the dawning half-light of the Renaissance: the first personal poet, and yet already mightier than any to come after. He joins teaching to art, art to feeling; he revives the art of antiquity in the element of emotion both personal and popular, and brings forth something vitally new. Everything that is most nobly human in the poetry of the people is to be found in him; but he has capacities that no one before or after him ever matched. . . . If one remove the priestly aura from his prodigious mystical poem and lay aside its doctrinal intention, there remains supremely great civil and human poetry; and the name of the divine poet of the Italian people takes flight into the future like the glory of the Campidoglio and the name of Rome.

Michele Barbi

Genesis and Composition of the *Divine Comedy*

THE earliest idea of what was Dante's greatest work stems doubtless from the plan to exalt Beatrice. The *Vita Nuova* ends with this promise: "There appeared to me a wonderful vision wherein I saw things which made me determine to say nothing more of this blessed one until I could more worthily speak of her; and for this reason I study all I can, as she truly knows. Wherefore, if it be His pleasure, in whom all things live, that my life endure a few more years, I hope to say of her what has never been said before of any woman."

It is useless to conjecture what he intended to do at that time and to ask whether anything might actually have been written with that plan in mind. He could not, however, forget so solemn a promise, not even in those years during which studies, politics, and the first worries of exile demanded his whole attention. When the plan was actually revived in his mind and to what years the composition of the poem may be traced are two questions which have been long and subtly discussed. Some writers, admitting that Dante had been thinking for some time of the *Commedia* and was steadily preparing the subject matter of it, maintain that he did not begin its composition until after the death of Henry VII. According to others, however, composition may have been started about the year 1307; so that the first two canticles were probably finished before the death of Henry or shortly after, and only the *Paradiso* occupied the last years of the poet's life. This second opinion seems more probable; we have sure proof that

before April, 1314, it was already possible to speak of a work "quod dicitur Comedia, et de infernalibus inter cetera multa tractat," as of a work, in part at least, generally known and therefore published. There are other indications; and, moreover, Dante himself, in the first eclogue, attests that, before the *Paradiso* was completed, the other two canticles had already been circulated. ("Quum mundi circumflua corpora cantu / astricolaeque meo, velut infera regna, patebunt.") [1] This makes it very likely that the *Inferno* and the *Purgatorio* had been published, if not together, at least only a brief time apart, shortly after the death of Henry. It may actually be that in 1306, while he was at the court of the Malaspina family, he received from Florence parts of a work that he had written there in praise of Beatrice. It may also be that the hard experience of exile forewarned him of the scant effect that a purely doctrinal treatise might have in healing the wounds of Italy. Perhaps his poetic nature, constrained and mortified by the hard discipline of philosophy and learning, regained, at a certain moment, the upper hand. It is probable that toward the year 1307 the idea of a work in verse came with the force of sheer necessity to his mind; a work which, over many years, had hauntingly whirled round and round in his spirit; a poem that would give expression to his memories, desires, experiences, ideas,

[1] *Ecl.*, I, 48–49. "When the wheeling planets of the universe and the dwellers of the stars shall be shown forth, as are already the lower kingdoms, in my song . . ."

From M. Barbi, *Life of Dante*, translated and edited by Paul G. Ruggiers, Berkeley and Los Angeles, University of California Press, 1954; reprinted by permission of the publisher.

hopes. In it he would attempt to reform humanity and particularly Italy, which was steadily moving away from the ideal of a truly political and Christian life.

Just as Aeneas had been destined by divine providence to prepare the birth of Rome and her universal Empire, and the apostle Paul had been chosen to spread the Christian Faith among the peoples, so Dante, afire with the idea of his great poem, will feel himself called upon to show the ravages brought about by the lack of the two guides appointed by God for the welfare of men, and to prophesy divine aid so that the divine plan may be restored. Civil honors, the care of earthly goods, shall revert to the Empire; the Church, free of duties which are not hers, shall resume the mission for which she was founded, shall guide men to heaven opened again to them by the sacrifice of Christ. Meanwhile he will present himself as an example of a man who returns to the truly religious life after recognizing the vanity of earthly goods. With the disappearance of the woman who had guided him "upon the right path" to love, the highest good, he became engrossed by temporal matters and started to travel down the road to perdition; but being a devout son of Mary, a loyal friend of justice, and a friend of Beatrice, he was not to die. The visit to the three realms of the other world under the guidance of Virgil sent by Beatrice, the guidance of Beatrice herself, the year of the great jubilee of 1300, all these shall make his soul whole again and render him worthy to reveal what God has arranged for the salvation of all mankind. Thus the plan of the poem born in exile, directed to a nobly social and religious end, is joined with the early idea of a work in which the poet would say of Beatrice what had never been said of any other woman.

It is not possible to trace the history of the composition of the poem in its successive phases during the ten and more years that it went on. The critics who have tried to do so, in their desire to be exact, have fallen into subtle and arbitrary conjectures. The beginnings were perhaps more modest than the whole poem indicates. Although the style was from the very outset what might be expected in a work that was to be called a *Commedia,* with its meter derived from the popular *serventese,* little by little Dante's artistic conscience made him feel that he could enter into competition with the great Latin poets.[2] His inspiration became progressively more elevated in tone, more consciously artistic,[3] until what was at first a "comedy" became a "sacred poem" for which neither the middle style nor the most common language sufficed; its style itself led to an early division of the work into three parts; and the numbers "three" and "ten" (two numbers of special significance for Dante, one as a symbol of the Trinity, the other as the symbol of perfection, according to the ideas of the age) became the regulating principle of the moral architecture of the three kingdoms, both in that first embryonic structure which is indispensable for every conception, poetic or otherwise, and in that successive elaboration of ideas and creation with which inspiration finally reaches its destined form. Thus we find three canticles for the three otherworldly realms, Inferno, Purgatory, Paradise; each canticle in thirty-three cantos, with one canto as an introduction to the entire poem, totaling exactly one hundred, multiple of ten. The Inferno, a vast abyss in the center of the earth, is divided into nine circles, plus the vestibule; there are as many divisions for the realm of purgation, a high mountain which rises from the midst of the ocean in the southern hemisphere, with the terrestrial Paradise at its peak; nine heavens, according to the Ptolemaic system, plus the empyrean, constitute Paradise. The sinners are arranged in the Inferno according as their sin stems from incontinence, violence, or fraud. The penitents in Purgatory are distributed according to whether their love

[2] *Inf.,* XXV, 94–102.
[3] *Purg.,* IX, 70–72.

is directed toward evil, or if directed toward good, with too much or too little zeal. The spirits of Paradise are divided into *saeculares, activi,* and *contemplativi,* according to whether their worldly passions perturbed their love of God, or whether this love expressed itself in the active or the contemplative life. The metrical device is the chain-linked tercet. As soon as the inspiration found its form, the whole was planned with consummate precision. The three canticles have almost the same number of lines, and each canticle ends with the word "stars." Such facts are external, but noteworthy, evidence of a most felicitous and powerful genius that could combine the most sublime and burning inspiration with rigorous meditation and minute craftsmanship of form.

Benedetto Croce

Aesthetic Criteria

To SAY, as has often been said (and I read it again in an American book), that Dante would burn with disdain for his greatest admirers and critics of the present day, for De Sanctis and Symonds, who were only affected by the sensible and poetical beauty of his work, is not an argument against, but rather in favour of a criticism which has covered a long distance from the days of Dante to our own. The aesthetic and the criticism which he practised in the ways then possible, were his affair; what we practise should be our affair.

But what is to be the aesthetic criterion we are to follow? If criticism in general has progressed, and with it the criticism of Dante, from the Middle Ages through the age of Romanticism to that of Idealism, can we still accept today the criterion that was formed in the last of these periods? It was certainly and without doubt superior to that of the neo-classic period. Notwithstanding that it brought much of the past in its train, it was able to place poetry at the summit of things in the world of the spirit, and Dante in the world of poetry. It could set him up as a perfect poetic genius and no longer as a teacher of doctrines, exhorter to virtue, or learned man of letters. Yet its aesthetic interpretation never succeeded in touching the right point, when determining the nature of art. It oscillated without arriving at a definition between the two extremes of a symbolical and a strongly realistic representation of the Idea or Cosmos.

Among certain critics, especially Italian, the first extreme prevailed. In poetry, and in Dante, they celebrated loftiness of concept and high morality shown in solemn and splendid forms. But this was not the more modern, the richer or more weighty of the two tendencies. Romantic criticism inclined to the other extreme, owing to the influence of contemporary currents opposed to the old classicist, didactic, oratorical, and rhetorical literature. It set great store by passion. Now passion is without doubt the very stuff of poetry and of art in general, and without passion poetry and art do not appear. But the romantics often confounded, on the one hand, passion as "material," with passion as "form," thus lowering the ideality of art, and on the other hand conceived passion as material in a restricted and arbitrary sense. They believed, for instance, that they could not find true passion outside certain confused, agitated, or violent forms and tones of passion, shot through with flashes of illumination serving only to deepen gloom and add exasperation to fury. They believed that this ideal was attained in the plays of Shakespeare and in certain of Goethe's characters, such as Werther, Faust, Mephistopheles, and Margaret, and in the poems and plays of Byron and of lesser writers. The result was that other tones and forms of passion, such for example as those expressive of security of thought, calm firmness of will, moderated energy, virtue, faith, and the like, were held to be less poetical or altogether unpoetical because they were (in the opinion of these critics) without conflict, that is to say, conflict in the sense above described.

The result also followed, unconnected with the former, but nevertheless psychologically explainable and proved true by the later fusion of Romanticism in Verism, that a tendency sprang up to conceive of art as a reproduction of reality, of a reality that is itself arbitrarily limited, gross, tangible, and strident.

The proper criticism of Dante's poetry has been obscured in several places by these aesthetic preconceptions and predilections of the Romantics. If they did not invent, they at least gave nourishment and vigour to the common belief that the poem of the "Inferno" is poetically superior to the other two, since it is that in which the human passions find their place, whereas they lose somewhat of their force and relief in the "Purgatorio" and vanish away altogether in the "Paradiso." In the "Inferno," too, we find concreteness and poetry and in the "Paradiso" only an insipid spectacle of beatitude. To this can be added the other judgment that the great poetic characters are to be met with in the first half of the "Inferno" and that we gradually descend to less dramatic sinners, until we reach "prose." To these critics, also, is due the condemnation of the doctrinal parts of the "Comedy" as prose in verse or as didacticism. To them also (I mention only the principal errors), is traceable the affirmation that Dante was well equipped to describe Hell, for which he was easily able to find a model in earthly life, but was bound to fail in the representation of Paradise without the aid of observation and experience. Schopenhauer among others repeated this statement, in order to obtain from it confirmation of his pessimistic judgment of the world, which was perfectly capable of being represented in an Inferno, but never in a Paradiso; and Leopardi had already remarked something similar in his "Zibaldone."

What little of truth some of these judgments contain will be seen in the proper places, but it is quite certain that they contain a great deal more of falsity, and that arguments about how much is false and true in them are generally in support of untenable theories. Take the theory, for instance, of the arbitrary restriction of the sphere of the passions, or that of the representability of Hell but not of Paradise. Truly, as regards the latter, Dante knew what his critics do not know or have forgotten, that Hell, Purgatory and Paradise, all modes of life beyond the grave, are neither representable nor conceivable by man. He intended only to give symbolical or allegorical representations. Constant and eternal torment surpasses the capacity of the human mind no less than constant and eternal joy. They are both unthinkable, because both are contradictory and absurd. But setting this aside, and assuming that all these three kingdoms are to be found somewhere on earth, they would nevertheless always be an external reality, the object or rather the work of naturalistic observation and of the classifying intellect, and unattainable for art, which draws not things but sentiments, or rather, creates its lofty imagery upon the sentiments. Not to speak of Paradise, it is impossible to draw artistically a rose or a cloud if imagination does not first transform sentiment into either rose or cloud.

With this statement we have already foreshadowed the criticism which is to take the place of the idealistic and romantic aesthetic, and which is in certain respects its correction and refutation. It embodies the conception of art as lyric or as lyrical intuition, a speculative conception to be kept distinct from the empirical conception of lyricism. During the disputes as to what literary class the "Divine Comedy" belongs to, the dramatic, the didactic, or a mixture of all, the "lyrical" has sometimes been suggested. But the lyricism of which we speak is not a kind of poetry; it is poetry itself; it is every work of art, whether it be called painting, architecture, sculpture, or music. It has nothing to do with the immediate outflow of feeling, and in the case of Dante with the expression of his "subjectivity," his character, or practical personality, as others have asserted and attempted to prove. It is an idea introduced by the new criticism to solve the antitheses that burdened the idealistic and romantic aesthetic. This rightly desired to seek a substance for art, but ended by finding it in external reality and in a new sort of "imitation of nature." It was right in seeking a theoretic form, but ended by finding it in a symbol, or sensible presentation of a speculative concept, thought or half-thought. The new criticism attempts to solve these antitheses by taking practical sentiment as material and by the elevation of sentiment to intuition as form, or to the rank of a theoretic problem which art both sets itself and solves with the creation of the image. The blame that has been put upon it for having reduced art to the echo-ing of passion, and for promoting ultra-Romanticism, is undeserved and does not require refutation, for it is evident that only by this new synthesis can the old antithesis between romantic and classic be overcome. It can further be shown that the use made to-day of the words "lyrical," "lyricism," "lyricity," by artists lacking both order and harmony, is the romantic caricature and perversion of a non-romantic conception, which originally appeared as a correction of Romanticism.

The methodological principles which I have been explaining are not confined to the study of Dante alone. They clearly extend to every kind of poetry and art. But they are those which it is most useful to bear in mind when attempting to remove the chief difficulties in which the criticism of Dante has been and still is involved.

Luigi Malagoli

The Substantive Penchant

DANTE has a leaning for the substantive. Without themselves being especially conspicuous in his writing, nouns influence its whole texture. And they do so without detriment to the adjectives: the two are found in harmonious equilibrium. But a secret tendency always urges for the transformation of adjectives, adverbs, and participles into nouns. Frequently it is the adverbial expression which is substantized, as in:

Sovra i fiori ond'è là giù adorno

(Over the flowers with which *there* is adorned)
Purg. IX, 54

where *là giù* (there) is used as grammatical subject. Tommaseo remarks on this passage that "the adverb used as a noun is a common occurrence in Tuscany"; which is true, but wants following up with a study of what Dante achieves with this usage. In another example:

Libero è *qui* da ogni alterazione

(*Here* is free from all change)
Purg. XXI, 43

the use of *qui* (here) as subject of the verb makes for rapidity of expression and gives frontality and immediacy to the spatial definition.

Substantized adjectives and participles gain in concreteness and freedom from abstract ties:

là dove pareami prima *rotto*
pur come un *fesso* che muro diparte,

(there where first appeared *a break*[1] like *a crack*[2] that divides a wall,)
Purg. IX, 74–75

Substantized by the use of the neuter, adjective and participle become more sharply pictorial than their related nouns:

Intorno a lui parea *calcato* e *pieno*
di cavalieri. . . .

(About him there appeared a trampling[3] and crowd[4] of horsemen. . . .)
Purg. X, 79–80

This shift to the substantive is basic to Dante's style. It gives breadth and sensitivity to his utterance while bringing it back to its point of departure—namely, the constant penchant for *things*. In

Ben sapev'ei che volea dir lo muto;

(Well did he know what the mute desired to say;)
Purg. XIII, 76

the adjective in its neuter noun form gives the sense of a self-existent entity, *the being mute*. Of the same character is the periphrasis which gives such liveliness to Dante's pictures. See, for example:

tanto che pria lo scemo della luna
rigiunse al letto suo per ricorcarsi,

(so that, earlier, the waning of the moon returned to its bed to rest,)
Purg. X, 14–15

[1] Literally, *broken*. [2] Literally, *a cracked*.
[3] Literally, *trampled*. [4] Literally, *full*.

Translated by the editor from *Linguaggio e Poesia nella Divina Commedia*, Genova, Briano, 1949; used by permission of the publisher.

In *lo scemo della luna*, which is to say the waned moon, the moon is reduced to a part of itself. Again of the same character is the stressing of some single noun in order to achieve brevity of statement:

Dopo la tratta d'un sospiro amaro,

(After the drawing of a bitter sigh,)

Purg. XXXI, 31

Any analysis of this substantive penchant in Dante is bound to take note of his handling of the abstract noun. Here the leaning for *things* and the secret substantizing tendency make themselves apparent with notable persistence and power. The abstract in Dante possesses, as it were, a concrete humus from which the *things* spring up. The pure abstraction is transfigured—put to use as a concrete. Note, in the following passage, how *le distinzion* (literally, the distinctions) bears the meaning of *distinct essences:*

Li altri giron per varie differenze
le distinzion che dentro di sè hanno
dispongono a lor fini e lor semenze.

(The other circling bodies by various differentiatings dispose the distinct powers they have within themselves, unto their ends and to their fertilizings.[5]

Par. II, 118–20

And in this:

Nella mia mente fè subito caso
questo ch'io dico, sì come si tacque
la gloriosa vita di Tommaso,
per la similitudine che nacque
del suo parlare e di quel di Beatrice,

(In my mind this that I say at once presented itself when the glorious life of Thomas ceased speaking, through the similitude that sprang from his speech and from Beatrice's,)

Par. XIV, 4–8

the abstract *similitudine* means the *similar fact*[6] rather than abstract resemblance.

[5] The translation of P. H. Wicksteed from the Temple Classics edition is given here, since it illustrates the author's point by rendering *distinzion* as "distinct powers."—Ed.
[6] See the three preceding lines of the canto.—Ed.

And see *Paradiso* XV, 78, where *simiglianza* (resemblance) occurs with underlying concrete sense; and *Paradiso* XV, 83, where *disagguaglianza* (unequalness) is similarly treated.

In his use of the collective noun, too, Dante gives a concrete value to the abstract, often making it more striking and more concentrated than the concrete term proper.

E se mio frate questo antivedesse,
l'avara *povertà* di Catalogna
già fuggirìa perchè non gli offendesse;

(And if my brother had foreseen this, he would already flee the miserly *poverty* of Catalonia lest it do him harm;)

Par. VIII, 76–78

Here the qualities of the Catalonians acquire body in the abstraction (miserly poverty), and appear incorporated and active in it. . . .

It is not a mere leaven of the concrete that marks Dante's use of the abstract: it is a preponderance. And the abstract thus solidified and embodied is the goal of the process that has been set up by the substantive penchant. Remarkable phenomenon: Dante empties the abstract of its own proper quality and makes it the emblem of that personal and abundant concreteness in which it is caught up. As a result of this peculiarly Dantesque accentuation of the concrete by means of the abstract, we get a new kind of poetic representationalism:

La novità del suono e il grande lume
di lor cagion m'accesero un disìo
mai non sentito di cotanto acume.

(The newness of the sound and the great light kindled in me a desire of their cause never before felt with such sharpness.)

Par. I, 82–84

In this, the *newness of the sound* (the abstract term placing us strongly in the presence of the thing signified), together with the *great light,* generates the atmosphere of miracle that characterizes the poetry.

Elsewhere the abstract has an intensifying capacity:

Dietro li andai incontro alla nequizia
di quella legge il cui popolo usurpa,
per colpa de' pastor, vostra giustizia.

(Following him, I marched against the iniquity of that law whose people usurps, by fault of our pastors, your justice.
Par. XV, 142–44

Observe in the above how the meaning centers about the first abstraction (*nequizia:* iniquity); and how, even in the second (*vostra giustizia:* your justice), although it is not equally rich with meaning, a concrete value is suggested. For "your justice" is not abstract justice, but *that which is justly due you, your rights.* "Justice" has also another meaning in Dante, namely the "justicing" act, which may itself be unjust as well as just. This is exemplified in *Paradiso* XIX, 77: *ov'è questa giustizia che il condanna?* (where is the justice that condemns him?), where the abstraction is animated by the action attributed to it. And the same word may have still a third sense, namely the penalty to which one is justly sentenced: says the Abbot of San Zeno to Dante in apology for being unable to halt from the running penalty of sloth:

però perdona
se villania nostra giustizia tieni.

(. . . therefore forgive if our penance seems rudeness.)
Purg. XVIII, 116–17

Here *justice* has an extremely concentrated and concrete sense that lies between the statement of a fact (the penalty) and the judgment of that penalty (that it is a just one); it is for this very reason coherent with Dante's style, and makes me disinclined to accept Tommaseo's interpretation of this *giustizia* as signifying love of the good.

Generally speaking, Dante uses the abstract to gain expressive force and concentration. In

Le sue *magnificenze* conosciute
saranno ancora sì che 'suoi nemici
non ne potran tener le lingue mute.

(His *munificences* shall still be known so that not even his enemies will be able to remain silent about them.)
Par. XVII, 85–87

the life of the passage springs from the motif of munificence expressed by an abstract term standing for a concrete ("munificences" for "munificent deeds") in a very vigorous opening.

This vigorous suggestion of the concrete through an abstract terminology is matched by Dante's use of another type of noun, not truly an abstract, but very wide in its denotative range, and therefore capable of the same sort of employment:

Ditemi, dunque, cara mia *primizia*
quai fur li vostri antichi, . . .

(Tell me, then, dear *firstling*, what was your ancestry, . . .)
Par. XVI, 22–23

Primizia is a noun of wide meaning (firstfruits, root-stock) used here to reinforce the particular, concrete reference.[7] It heightens and concentrates the value of the meaning implicit in it (progenitor, first father), and at the same time amplifies it. The same may be said of its use in *Paradiso* XXV, 14–15, where, in "la primizia che lascio Cristo de' vicari suoi" (the first-fruit, of his vicars, left by Christ) the term, followed by the specification *of his vicars,* reinforces the firstness of the apostle Peter. . . .

ALOGICALITY AND CONCENTRATION

In addition to giving concrete value to abstract terms and favoring the substantive form, Dante's penchant for *things* leads to a characteristic use of adjectives: they be-

[7] Dante is here addressing his own ancestor, Cacciaguida.—Ed.

come self-subsistent and active; they stand out in the sentence as points of substantive concentration and stress.

> Quelli che vedi qui furon *modesti*
> a riconoscer sè dalla bontade
> che li avea fatti a tanto intender presti.

> (Those you see here were *modest* to acknowledge themselves (created) by the good that made them quick to such understanding.)
> Par. XXIX, 58–60

In this passage the linking of *modesti* (modest) with *a riconoscer* (to recognize) is not only logical, but pictorial: what the phrase conveys is that these souls held back, they hesitated to make their recognition; and the adjective gives greater concreteness to the pictured action than the rendering by means of a verb could do. The same is true of

> Quelle sustanze poi che fur *gioconde*
> della faccia di Dio. . . .

> (These substances, since they became *joyous* before the face of God. . . .)
> Par. XXIX, 76–77

where the adjective gives us the act of rejoicing with great immediacy. . . .

But this love of things that characterizes Dante's speech is surely felt most strongly in the attenuation of the logical groundwork and in the strong presence of things, themselves. Conceptual matter never intrudes upon Dante's style, enfeebling it or stretching it for the sake of logical completeness. And this is not so much a result of stylistic intention as of mental attitude—of distaste for *intarsio* and logical harmonies. Modern writers have a more scrupulous and urgent sense of logical completeness and coherence; they have, as a result of the modern taste for indirection, a greater detachment from real things. And this comes of the prevalence of reason over the immediate sense of reality. It is his fundamental attitude that makes the visible hold first place and logic last in Dante's writing. It is this that leads him to make logical relations visible and to replace logical with spatial definition. . . .

Such is the substantive penchant in Dante, and such the structure of his sentences, geared entirely to *things*, requiring no mediating terminology. It seems to me wrong to say that his taste for the spatial criterion or for geometric order constitutes "a predominance of scientific habit over poetic inspiration"; [8] within the orbit of language every kind of expression contributes to an understanding of Dante's feeling for and portrayal of reality. His avoidance of the logical approach is merely one of the traits of his expressive sensibility, and is born of an intimate need. His concreteness is his mental garb; his tendency towards non-logical, close-knit expression flows from his immediate penchant for reality, and links his language tightly to the things of sense, themselves.

[8] A. Momigliano, *Commento al Purgatorio* (Florence, 1946), p. 335.

Erich Auerbach

Figural Art in the *Divine Comedy* [1]

THE figural interpretation, or to put it more completely, the figural view of history was widespread and deeply influential up to the Middle Ages, and beyond. This has not escaped the attention of scholars. Not only theological works on the history of hermeneutics but also studies on the history of art and literature have met with figural conceptions on their way, and dealt with them. This is particularly true of the history of art in connection with medieval iconography, and of the history of literature in connection with the religious theater of the Middle Ages. But the special nature of the problem does not seem to have been recognized; the figural or typological or phenomenal structure is not sharply distinguished from other, allegorical or symbolical, forms. A beginning is to be found in T. C. Goode's instructive dissertation on Gonzalo de Berceo's *El Sacrificio de la Misa* (Washington, 1933); although he does not go into fundamental questions,

[1] The following pages are excerpted and re-titled from Part IV of a four-part essay entitled "Figura." The earlier sections deal with the history of the Latin "figura" and with the nature of early Christian figural interpretation of sacred texts, distinguishing figural art sharply from allegory by reason of its characteristic use of essentially concrete and historic terms, and its avoidance of generality and abstraction. Important for the reader of the pages on Dante is the following definition in Part III: "Figural interpretation establishes a connection between two events or persons, the first of which signifies not only itself but also the second, while the second encompasses or fulfills the first. The two poles of the figure are separate in time, but both, being real events or figures, are within time, within the stream of historical life."—Ed.

H. Pflaum shows a clear understanding of the situation in his *Die religiöse Disputation in der europäischen Dichtung des Mittelalters* (Geneva-Florence, 1935). Recently (in *Romania*, LXIII) his sound understanding of the word *figure* enabled him to give a correct interpretation of some Old French verses that had been misunderstood by the editor and to restore the text. Perhaps other examples have escaped me, but I do not think that there is any systematic treatment of the subject. Yet such an investigation strikes me as indispensable for an understanding of the mixture of spirituality and sense of reality which characterizes the European Middle Ages and which seems so baffling to us. In most European countries figural interpretation was active up to the eighteenth century; we find traces of it not only in Bossuet as might be expected, but many years later in the religious authors whom Groethuysen quotes in *Les Origines de la France bourgeoise*. A clear knowledge of its character and how it differed from related but differently structured forms would generally sharpen and deepen our understanding of the documents of late antiquity and the Middle Ages, and solve a good many puzzles. Might the themes that recur so frequently on early Christian sarcophagi and in the catacombs not be figures of the Resurrection? Or to cite an example from Mâle's great work, might not the legend of Maria Aegyptiaca, the representations of which in the Toulouse Museum he describes (op. cit., p. 240 ff.), be a figure of the people of Israel going out of Egypt, hence to be interpreted exactly as the Psalm *In exitu Israel de Aegypto* was generally interpreted in the Middle Ages?

But individual interpretations do not exhaust the importance of the figural method. No student of the Middle Ages can fail to see how it provides the medieval interpretation of history with its general foundation and often enters into the medieval view of everyday reality. The analogism that reaches into every sphere of medieval thought is closely bound up with the figural structure; in the interpretation of the Trinity that extends roughly from Augustine's *De Trinitate* to St. Thomas, I, q. 45, art. 7, man himself, as the image of God, takes on the character of a *figura Trinitatis*. It is not quite clear to me how far aesthetic ideas were determined by figural conceptions—to what extent the work of art was viewed as the *figura* of a still unattainable fulfillment in reality. The question of the imitation of nature in art aroused little theoretical interest in the Middle Ages; but all the more attention was accorded to the notion that the artist, as a kind of figure for God the Creator, realized an archetype that was alive in his spirit. These, as we see, are ideas of Neoplatonic origin. But the question remains: to what extent were this archetype and the work of art produced from it regarded as figures for a reality and truth fulfilled in God? I have found no conclusive answer in the texts available to me here and the most important works of the specialized literature are lacking. But I should like to quote a few passages which happen to be at hand, and which point somewhat in the direction I have in mind. In an article on the representation of musical tones in the capitals of the Abbey of Cluny (*Deutsche Vierteljahrsschrift*, 7, p. 264) L. Schrade quotes an explanation of the word *imitari* by Remigius of Auxerre: *scilicet persequi, quia veram musicam non potest humana musica imitari* ("that is, to follow after, for the music of man cannot imitate the true music"). This is probably based on

the notion that the artist's work is an imitation or at least a shadowy figuration of a true and likewise sensuous reality (the music of the heavenly choirs). In the *Purgatorio* Dante praises the works of art created by God himself, representing examples of virtues and vices, for their perfectly fulfilled sensuous truth, beside which human art and even nature pales (*Purg.*, 10 and 12); his invocation to Apollo (*Par.*, 1) includes the lines:

> O divina virtù, se mi ti presti
> tanto che l'ombra del beato regno
> segnata nel mio capo io manifesti

> (O divine Virtue, if thou dost so far lend thyself
> to me, that I make manifest the shadow of
> the blessed realm imprinted on my brain.
> (Temple Classics ed., p. 5.)

Here his poetry is characterized as an *umbra* of truth, engraved in his mind, and his theory of inspiration is sometimes expressed in statements that may be explained along the same lines. But these are only suggestions; an investigation purporting to explain the relation between Neoplatonic and figural elements in medieval aesthetics would require broader foundations. Still, the present remarks suffice, I believe, to show the need for distinguishing the figural structure from the other forms of imagery. We may say roughly that the figural method in Europe goes back to Christian influences, while the allegorical method derives from ancient pagan sources, and also that the one is applied primarily to Christian, the other to ancient material. Nor shall we be going too far afield in terming the figural view the predominantly Christian-medieval one, while the allegorical view, modeled on pagan or not inwardly Christianized authors of late antiquity, tends to appear where ancient, pagan, or strongly secular influences are dominant. But such observations are too general and imprecise, for the many phenomena that reflect an intermingling of different cultures over a thousand years do not admit of such simple classifications. At a very early date profane and pagan material was also interpreted figurally; Gregory of Tours, for example, uses the legend of the Seven Sleepers as a figure for the Resurrection; the waking of Lazarus from the dead and Jonah's rescue from the belly of the whale were also commonly interpreted in this sense. In the high Middle Ages, the Sybils, Virgil, the characters of the *Aeneid*, and even those of the Breton legend cycle (e.g., Galahad in the quest for the Holy Grail) were drawn into the figural interpretation, and moreover there were all sorts of mixtures between figural, allegoric, and symbolic forms. All these forms, applied to classical as well as Christian material, occur in the work which concludes and sums up the culture of the Middle Ages: the *Divine Comedy*. But I shall now attempt to show that basically it is the figural forms which predominate and determine the whole structure of the poem.

At the foot of the mountain of Purgatory, Dante and Virgil meet a man of venerable mien, whose countenance is illumined by four stars signifying the four cardinal virtues. He inquires sternly into the legitimacy of their journey and from Virgil's respectful reply—after he has told Dante to kneel before this man—we learn that it is Cato of Utica. For after explaining his divine mission, Virgil continues as follows (*Purg.*, 1, 70–5):

Or ti piaccia gradir la sua venuta:
  libertà va cercando, che è sì cara,
  come sa chi per lei vita rifiuta.
Tu il sai, chè non ti fu per lei amara
  in Utica la morte, ove lasciasti
  la vesta che al gran dì sarà sì chiara.

(Now may it please thee to be gracious unto his coming: he seeketh freedom, which is so precious, as he knows who giveth up life for her.
Thou knowest it; since for her sake death was not bitter to thee in Utica, where thou leftest the raiment which at the great day shall be so bright.)

Temple Classics ed., p. 7.)

Virgil goes on, asking Cato to favor him for the sake of the memory of Marcia, his former wife. This plea Cato rejects with undiminished severity; but if such is the desire of the *donna del ciel* (Beatrice), that suffices; and he orders that before his ascent Dante's face be cleansed of the stains of Hell and that he be girded with reeds. Cato appears again at the end of the second canto, where he sternly rebukes the souls just arrived at the foot of the mountain, who are listening in self-forgetfulness to Casella's song, and reminds them to get on with their journey.

It is Cato of Utica whom God has here appointed guardian at the foot of Purgatory: a pagan, an enemy of Caesar, and a suicide. This is startling, and the very first commentators, such as Benvenuto of Imola, expressed their bewilderment. Dante mentions only a very few pagans who were freed from Hell by Christ; and among them we find an enemy of Caesar, whose associates, Caesar's murderers, are with Judas in the jaws of Lucifer, who as a suicide seems no less guilty than those others "who have done themselves violence" and who for the same sin are suffering the most frightful torments in the seventh circle of Hell. The riddle is solved by the words of Virgil, who says that Dante is seeking freedom, which is so precious as you yourself know who have despised life for its sake. The story of Cato is removed from its earthly and political context, just as the stories of Isaac, Jacob, etc., were removed from theirs by the patristic exegetes of the Old Testament, and made into a *figura futurorum*. Cato is a *figura*, or rather the earthly Cato, who renounced his life for freedom, was a *figura*, and the Cato who appears here in the *Purgatorio* is the revealed or fulfilled figure, the truth of that figural event. The political and earthly freedom for which he died was only an *umbra futurorum*: a prefiguration of the Christian freedom whose guardian he is here appointed, and for the sake of which he here again opposes all earthly temptation; the Christian freedom from all evil impulses, which leads to true domination of self, the freedom for the acquisition of which Dante is girded with the rushes of humility, until, on the summit of the mountain, he actually achieves it and is crowned by Virgil as lord over himself. Cato's voluntary choice of death rather than political servitude is here introduced as a *figura* for the eternal freedom of the children of God, in behalf of which all earthly things are to be despised, for the liberation of the soul from the servitude of sin. Dante's choice of Cato for this role is explained by the position "above the parties" that Cato occupies according to the Roman authors, who held him up as a model of virtue, justice, piety, and love of freedom. Dante found him praised equally in Cicero, Virgil, Lucan, Seneca, and Valerius Maximus; particularly Virgil's *secretosque pios his dantem iura Catonem* (*Aeneid*, 8, 670) ("the righteous in a place apart, with Cato their lawgiver"), coming as it did from a poet of the Empire, must have made a great impression on him. His admiration for Cato may be judged from several passages in the *Convivio*, and in his *De Monarchia* (2, 5) he has a quotation from Cicero saying that Cato's voluntary death should be judged in a special light and connecting it with the examples of Roman political virtue to which Dante attached so much importance; in this passage Dante tries to show that Roman rule was legitimized by Roman virtue; that it fostered the justice and freedom of all mankind. The chapter contains this sentence: *Romanum imperium de fonte nascitur pietatis* ("the Roman Empire springs from the fount of justice").

Dante believed in a predetermined concordance between the Christian story of salvation and the Roman secular monarchy; thus it is not surprising that he should apply the figural interpretation to a pagan Roman—in general he draws his symbols, allegories, and figures from both worlds without distinction. Beyond any doubt Cato is a *figura;* not an allegory like the characters from the *Roman de la Rose,* but a figure that has become the truth. The *Comedy* is a vision which regards and proclaims the figural truth as already fulfilled, and what constitutes its distinctive character is precisely that, fully in the spirit of figural interpretation, it attaches the truth perceived in the vision to historical, earthly events. The character of Cato as a severe, righteous, and pious man, who in a significant moment in his own destiny and in the providential history of the world sets freedom above life, is preserved in its full historical and personal force; it does not become an allegory for freedom; no, Cato of Utica stands there as a unique individual, just as Dante saw him; but he is lifted out of the tentative earthly state in which he regarded political freedom as the highest good (just as the Jews singled out strict observance of the Law), and transposed into a state of definitive fulfillment, concerned no longer with the earthly works of civic virtue or the law, but with the *ben dell'intelletto,* the highest good, the freedom of the immortal soul in the sight of God.

Let us attempt the same demonstration in a somewhat more difficult case. Virgil has been taken by almost all commentators as an allegory for reason—the human, natural reason which leads to the right earthly order, that is, in Dante's view, the secular monarchy. The older commentators had no objection to a purely allegorical interpretation, for they did not, as we do today, feel that allegory was incompatible with authentic poetry. Many modern critics have argued against this idea, stressing the poetic, human, personal quality of Dante's Virgil; still, they have been unable either to deny that he "means something" or to find a satisfactory relation between this meaning and the human reality. Recently (and not only in connection with Virgil) a number of writers (L. Valli and Mandonnet, for example) have gone back to the purely allegorical or symbolic aspect and attempted to reject the historical reality as "positivistic" or "romantic." But actually there is no choice between historical and hidden meaning; both are present. The figural structure preserves the historical event while interpreting it as revelation; and must preserve it in order to interpret it.

In Dante's eyes the historical Virgil is both poet and guide. He is a poet and a guide because in the righteous Aeneas' journey to the underworld he prophesies and glorifies universal peace under the Roman Empire, the political order which Dante regards as exemplary, as the *terrena Jerusalem*; and because in his poem the founding of Rome, predestined seat of the secular and spiritual power, is celebrated in the light of its future mission. Above all he is poet and guide because all the great poets who came after him have been inflamed and inspired by his work; Dante not only states this for himself, but brings in a second poet, Statius, to proclaim the same thing most emphatically: in the meeting with Sordello and perhaps also in the highly controversial verse about Guido Cavalcanti (*Inf.*, 10, 63) the same theme is sounded. In addition, Virgil is a guide because, beyond his temporal prophecy, he also—in the Fourth Eclogue—proclaimed the eternal transcendent order, the appearance of Christ which would usher in the renewal of the temporal world without, to be sure, suspecting the significance of his own words, but nevertheless in such a way that posterity might derive inspiration from his light. Virgil the poet was a guide because he had described the realm of the dead—thus he knew the way thither. But also as a Roman and a man, he was destined to be a guide, for not only was he a master of eloquent discourse and lofty wisdom but also possessed the qualities that fit a man for guidance and leadership, the qualities that characterize his hero Aeneas and Rome in general: *iustitia* and *pietas*. For Dante the historical Virgil embodied this fullness of earthly perfection and was therefore capable of guiding him

to the very threshold of insight into the divine and eternal perfection; the historic Virgil was for him a *figura* of the poet-prophet-guide, now fulfilled in the other world. The historical Virgil is "fulfilled" by the dweller in limbo, the companion of the great poets of antiquity, who at the wish of Beatrice undertakes to guide Dante. As a Roman and poet Virgil had sent Aeneas down to the underworld in search of divine counsel to learn the destiny of the Roman world; and now Virgil is summoned by the heavenly powers to exercise a no less important guidance; for there is no doubt that Dante saw himself in a mission no less important than that of Aeneas: elected to divulge to a world out of joint the right order, which is revealed to him upon his way. Virgil is elected to point out and interpret for him the true earthly order, whose laws are carried out and whose essence is fulfilled in the other world, and at the same time to direct him toward its goal, the heavenly community of the blessed, which he has presaged in his poetry—yet not into the heart of the kingdom of God, for the meaning of his presage was not revealed to him during his earthly lifetime, and without such illumination he has died an unbeliever. Thus God does not wish Dante to enter His kingdom with Virgil's help; Virgil can lead him only to the threshold of the kingdom, only as far as the limit which his noble and righteous poetry was able to discern. "Thou first," says Statius to Virgil, "didst send me towards Parnassus to drink in its caves, and then didst light me on to God. Thou didst like one who goes by night, and carries the light behind him, and profits not himself, but maketh persons wise that follow him. . . . Through thee I was a poet, through thee a Christian." [2] And just as the earthly Virgil led Statius to salvation, so now, as a fulfilled figure, he leads Dante: for Dante too has received from him the lofty style of poetry, through him he is

[2] *Purg.* XXII, 69–73, Temple Classics ed.

saved from eternal damnation and set on the way of salvation; and just as he once illumined Statius, without himself seeing the light that he bore and proclaimed, so now he leads Dante to the threshold of the light, which he knows of but may not himself behold.

Thus Virgil is not an allegory of an attribute, virtue, capacity, power, or historical institution. He is neither reason nor poetry nor the Empire. He is Virgil himself. Yet he is not himself in the same way as the historical characters whom later poets have set out to portray in all their historical involvement, as for example, Shakespeare's Caesar or Schiller's Wallenstein. These poets disclose their historical characters in the thick of their earthly existence; they bring an important epoch to life before our eyes, and look for the meaning of the epoch itself. For Dante the meaning of every life has its place in the providential history of the world, the general lines of which are laid down in the Revelation which has been given to every Christian, and which is interpreted for him in the vision of the *Comedy*. Thus Virgil in the *Divine Comedy* is the historical Virgil himself, but then again he is not; for the historical Virgil is only a *figura* of the fulfilled truth that the poem reveals, and this fulfillment is more real, more significant than the *figura*. With Dante, unlike modern poets, the more fully the figure is interpreted and the more closely it is integrated with the eternal plan of salvation, the more real it becomes. And for him, unlike the ancient poets of the underworld, who represented earthly life as real and the life after death as shadow, for him the other world is the true reality, while this world is only *umbra futurorum*—though indeed the *umbra* is the prefiguration of the transcendent reality and must recur fully in it.

For what has been said here of Cato and Virgil applies to the *Comedy* as a whole. It is wholly based on a figural conception. In my study of Dante as a poet of the earthly world (1929) I attempted to show that in the *Comedy* Dante undertook "to conceive the whole earthly historical world . . . as already subjected to God's final judgment and thus put in its proper place as decreed by the divine judgment, to represent it as a world already judged . . . in so doing, he does not destroy or weaken the earthly nature of his characters, but captures the fullest intensity of their individual earthly-historical being and identifies it with the ultimate state of things" (p. 108). At that time I lacked a solid historical grounding for this view, which is already to be found in Hegel and which is the basis of my interpretation of the *Divine Comedy*; it is suggested rather than formulated in the introductory chapters of the book. I believe that I have now found this historical grounding; it is precisely the figural interpretation of reality which, though in constant conflict with purely spiritualist and Neoplatonic tendencies, was the dominant view in the European Middle Ages: the idea that earthly life is thoroughly real, with the reality of the flesh into which the Logos entered, but that with all its reality it is only *umbra* and *figura* of the authentic, future, ultimate truth, the real reality that will unveil and preserve the *figura*. In this way the individual earthly event is not regarded as a definite self-sufficient reality, nor as a link in a chain of development in which single events or combinations of events perpetually give rise to new events, but viewed primarily in immediate vertical connection with a divine order which encompasses it, which on some future day will itself be concrete reality; so that the earthly event is a prophecy or *figura* of a part of a wholly divine reality that will be enacted in the future. But this reality is not only future; it is always present in the eye of God and in the other world, which is to say that in transcendence the revealed and true reality is present at all times, or timelessly. Dante's work is an attempt to give a poetic and at the same time systematic picture of the world in this light. Divine grace comes to the help of a man menaced by earthly confusion and ruin—this is the framework of the vision. From early youth he had been favored by special grace, because he was destined for a special task; at an early age he had been privileged to see revelation incarnated in a living being, Beatrice—and here as so often figural structure and Neoplatonism are intertwined. In her lifetime she had, though covertly, favored him with a salutation of her eyes and mouth; and in dying she had distinguished him in an unspoken mysterious way. When he strays from the right path, the departed Beatrice, who for him was revelation incarnate, finds the only possible salvation for him; indirectly she is his guide and in Paradise directly; it is she who shows him the unveiled order, the truth of the earthly figures. What he sees and learns in the three realms is true, concrete reality, in which the earthly *figura* is contained and interpreted; by seeing the fulfilled truth while still alive, he himself is saved, while at the same time he is enabled to tell the world what he has seen and guide it to the right path.

Philip H. Wicksteed

Hell

DANTE himself tells us [1] that the "Comedy" is essentially a practical treatise, and is speculative only incidentally; and as we penetrate further into its spirit we realise more and more clearly that the real preoccupation of Dante's mind as he wrote the "Comedy" was neither scientific nor philosophical, but at once artistic and (in the fullest Hebrew sense) prophetic. The beginner is, of course, often dashed by the display of learning he finds in Dante and the demands made upon his own (probably non-existent) erudition; and the impression is often retained by more advanced students that Dante carries science and philosophy to the furthest limits which had been reached in his age. It is only after detailed study that we learn to appreciate the artistic tact and self-restraint with which he refrains from pushing his science, philosophy, or even theology, a step beyond the boundaries within which they can support his ethical, religious, and poetical purposes; and at the same time his boldness and independence in handling them, and the moulding ascendency of his own mind.

Thus in his astronomy he deliberately ignores, for the sake of simplicity and picturesque effect, the distinction between the constellations and the signs of the zodiac, although he was perfectly well aware of the cause of the discrepancy in what he thought of as the proper motion of the stars and what modern astronomy speaks of as the precession of the equinoxes. And I agree with Dr. Moore (though

not in detail) in his general thesis that the whole astronomical scheme of the "Comedy" is based on popular approximations (in the case of the moon an extremely rough one) which Dante knew to be scientifically incorrect. He used his science to give vividness and firmness to his pictorial presentation of the journey, carrying it just as far as he thought an educated man could follow without an appeal to books of reference, but no further. He did not use his pictorial presentations of the journey as an excuse for inveigling the reader into the study of the technical details of astronomy, and still less as an excuse for the display of his own learning.

And it is just the same with his theology, his philosophy, and his technical psychology. Perplexing as the uninitiated may sometimes find his treatment of these subjects, the student of Scholastic Philosophy will be impressed by the infallible instinct, or art, with which he abstains from pushing intellectual analysis to the point at which it would divert instead of stimulating the mind, and would obscure rather than illuminate moral and spiritual issues. He is content to accept the mystery of the Trinity, for example, without trying how far the plummet of the human mind can reach into the abyss of the infinite. He is content to look forward to the time when the union of the divine and human natures in the person of Christ shall be as obvious to the beatified vision as the axiomatic law of contradictories, and meanwhile to accept it by faith.

But there is more than this. Dante not

[1] Epistle to Can Grande, par. 16, lines 271–81.

From P. H. Wicksteed, *Dante and Aquinas*, London, J. M. Dent & Sons, 1913; reprinted by permission of the publisher.

only knows where to stop himself, but he knows where science stops. He knows that by trying to explain what is inexplicable you may not only fail, but may wrench the instrument of reason itself in the process. Such at least I take to be the meaning of that passage in the early part of the *Paradiso* which has dismayed so many readers by its apparently irrelevant intrusion into heaven. I mean the long and somewhat intricate disquisition on the dark portions of the surface of the moon. Dante's purpose evidently is to show that when he had left the earth one of the first lessons he had to learn was that if you try to explain the things of heaven by the laws of the laboratory you will not only fail in your attempt, but you will strain and violate the laws of the very science that you put to a task which is not its own. Your science will not only be ineffective as an instrument, but it will be bad as science.[2]

Nowhere are the happy effects of this self-restraint, or deliberate sense of the limits past which philosophy cannot go (whichever in this particular case it is), more happy than in Dante's treatment of what he regards as the central problem of the moral world, the freedom, namely, of the human will.

Aquinas and Dante are equally emphatic in their insistence on the fact of the freedom of the will. Without it the reality of the moral life disappears, rewards and punishments are impossible, and the very idea of divine justice perishes.

Many passages in the "Comedy" will occur to the reader's mind in which Dante dwells upon this theme. In one of his letters he speaks of the astrologer, who thinks that he can predict events, as in the highest degree blasphemous and injurious, because

he implies that man's actions are not under his own control, and that free will is illusory;[3] but the most striking illustration of all is in that early canto of the *Paradiso* in which Dante, having seen, in the Sphere of the Moon, certain nuns who had broken their vows "against their will" is haunted by two questions. The first is: If they were compelled to break their vows, does it accord with God's justice that they should be shorn of some portion of the bliss of fruition that they would otherwise have enjoyed? And the other is: Seeing that these inconstant souls (if such indeed they are) abide in the inconstant moon, can it be true, after all, that Plato is right in teaching that the souls derive their moral qualities from the planets from which they have descended into the human body, and that they afterwards revert to the planets from which they came? Beatrice sees these two perplexities in his mind, and also that he is at a loss which question to ask first, like a hare between two hounds not knowing which way to turn. So she says she will treat first of the one that has most poison in it. Now remember what these two questions are; one concerns the justice of God, and the other the relation of the planets to the origin and destiny of the soul. The one with most poison in it is the one about the planets. The other can wait. And this is because the question why these nuns lose a part of their glory only concerns a detail in God's administration. But if you are to suppose that a man's moral character is determined by the planet from which his soul comes and also that his future state is determined by his moral character, then you have undermined the very conception of divine justice itself, because you have undermined the conception of free will, on which the justice of the whole of God's ordinances rests.

Now Aquinas, as I have said, attaches the same importance to the free will, and

[2] It is perhaps a little unfortunate that in point of fact Dante's science as to the moon in the *Convivio* was on the whole a little better than Beatrice's in the *Paradiso* that corrects it. But that, of course, does not affect the principle that Dante is illustrating.

[3] *Epistle* viii. *Cardinalibus Italicis*, lines 38–41.

for the same reason. But there is this difference, that whereas Dante only carries his analysis to a certain point, Aquinas urges it to the very end; and the consequence is that whereas Dante's treatment of the subject is a perpetual appeal to our inherent sense that we are in command of our own destiny, and that neither the movements of the heavens nor any other combination of circumstances or events can rob us of the liberty which we have in God or take our fate out of our own hands, Aquinas, on the other hand, analyses the freedom of the will till he has analysed it away, and leaves us with the sense not that we are really and ultimately responsible for our own choice, but that we choose, even when we choose wrong, in obedience to the inevitable and unfathomable will of God.

It will be instructive to follow out this contrast between Aquinas and Dante. According to Aquinas man selects both his ends (subject to his controlling desire for blessedness[4]) and his means, and never takes one course rather than another except because he prefers it. Moreover, the action of man differs from the fixed and determined course of nature because it is regulated not by antecedents but by consequents. In the mechanical order the thing that happens is rigidly determined by the things that have happened, and is absolutely unaffected by what is going to happen as a consequent; whereas even in the animal world it is the anticipation of pleasure or of pain, that is to say, something which is going to happen, that determines the conduct of the brute in many respects. Moreover, man may imaginatively conceive of all kinds of possibilities which are not directly presented to him, and may select among them one towards which his action shall be directed. He is therefore free, in the sense that he is not bound down to a predetermined course by his past, or limited in his choice by the suggestions actually made by present things to his senses, but

is capable of selecting among a variety of open courses by considering the future. And seeing that he selects the one course or the other because he prefers it, he is not only free, but responsible in his freedom. If he chooses the evil course he chooses it because he prefers it, and he deserves the penalty attaching to this evil preference. He cannot say that he did it in spite of himself, because he chose to do it, and he chose to do it because he preferred it.

But when we push the inquiry further, and ask why of all these open alternatives he chooses the one rather than the other, we are assured indeed that although all kinds of predisposing causes may prompt or suggest the one course or the other, yet none of them can compel the choice. Neither physical habit nor any external influence, not even the movements of the heavens or the suggestions of demons, that raise all kinds of images in the imagination, nor the natural movements of the passions themselves, can have direct access to the will or can compel the choice by promptings or seductive suggestions. God alone can directly act upon the will, and either by prompting or refraining can determine the choice that it will make. But since God does prompt or refrain in every case the will actually makes its choice in obedience to the divine will. Thus after all, though Aquinas will never formulate it so, it amounts to this, that, although we do what we like, it is God that chooses what we shall like, and therefore it is he, not we, on whom the ultimate choice and its responsibility rest. What then comes of the freedom of the human will, undetermined by the past? Aquinas expressly states that it is in our power to will or not to will any action. Indeed he insists, in words, on the reality of the freedom of the will, so often and so emphatically, that many of his modern readers still insist that he is not a determinist. But their case is hopeless. On examination our power to will or not to will reduces itself to this: In the mechanical succession of material events only one consequent of any given set of antecedents is possible within the limits of the nature of the material thing concerned. If a stone is released in free air, nothing is possible within the limits of its nature except that it should fall towards the centre of the earth. God could indeed make it rise, but that would be by miracle, superseding the nature of the stone and making it act counter thereto. But in the case of man there is no such natural, internal determination of the future by the past. So far as the intrinsic nature of man is concerned diverse courses are open, and God could urge him or suffer him to move along any one of the diverse possible routes without any violation of his nature or breach with the natural continuity of past and future. The freedom of man resolves itself then into the existence of open possibilities within the range of his natural powers, and the determination of his course by his own preferences. But his preferences themselves are ultimately determined by God.

And this doctrine relentlessly pushed home reveals its appalling significance in relation to the Aquinian doctrine of hell. We have seen that God wills his own goodness, including the communication of his goodness to other beings. These other beings must of necessity be finite, for could we conceive of the Infinite creating the Infinite there would still be but one Infinite, and so there could be no communication of the divine self to any other being. The created beings then to whom the divine goodness communicates itself must be finite; and the communication must be made under finite conditions, that is to say, in diversity and not in unity. God then must reveal his supreme excellence both in the form under which we conceive it as mercy and the form under which we conceive it as justice. Justice must manifest itself by the infliction of penalties. Penalties are due only to those who have averted their love from the divine goodness to lower things and made the evil choice. If the revelation

of the divine goodness then is to be complete in its diversity, there must be material on which to demonstrate the divine justice. There must therefore be sin and hell. Thus hell is good, not in itself, but as an essential part of a good greater than its evil, the manifestation, namely, of God's goodness. What we call evil, therefore, is itself, from the higher point of view and in its connection and setting, good. The pains of hell are good, but with appalling candour Aquinas adds that they are not good for those who suffer them.

Thus we are bidden to think of the eternal hell, of impenitence and anguish, as involved and included in the act by which God wills his own goodness. Thomas pushes his explanation of the free will and his explanation of hell so far as to carry the latter into the very central will of God. He does not leave it as a mystery, but represents it as something that should approve itself to the human reason and sense of fitness.

Now note that Dante's treatment of the freedom of the will in the eighteenth canto of the *Purgatorio* is carried just to the point at which it removes the superficial objections, and no further. Both here and elsewhere he declares that the ineradicable feeling which every man has in his heart that he is indeed master of himself when he makes a deliberate choice is not an illusion. Suggestions cannot dominate him if he chooses to dominate them. Thus Dante's assertion of the doctrine of the free will is simply an appeal to our own direct consciousness of power, which it braces and strengthens in us. It so touches our manhood that we cannot for shame excuse ourselves by circumstance, or despair in the face of difficulty or opposition.

Thus Dante makes us feel that over a wide area of life, at any rate, man gets essentially not only what he deserves, but what he chooses; and that he neither deserves nor gets it except because he chooses it. And it is this conception of desert and choice that permeates Dante's whole treatment of the awful theme of the *Inferno*. Aquinas and Dante are at one in representing the damned as impenitent. The former repeatedly declares that they do not repent of their sins, but only hate their punishment. But yet he frequently speaks of the "worm" or "gnawing" of conscience as a part of their torment. And this gives us the impression that he did not hold with so firm a grasp as Dante did the full consequences of their common principle that there has been no change in the sinner's sense of moral values. This is an essential feature of Dante's hell. The souls still have just the same preferences that they had on earth. Their scale of values remains unchanged. It is not that their repentance is unavailing, but that they do not repent. They curse the parents who begat them, or the accomplices that seduced or betrayed them, never their own inherently evil choice, for they still cling to it. There is shame in Dante's hell as well as shamelessness, but surely there is no room for the gnawing worm of conscience there.

But so far the difference, if there really is one, between Dante and Aquinas, is hardly crucial; for all the principles that seem to exclude remorse from Dante's hell are fully accepted by Thomas. What really divides them is the moral relation in the thought of Dante, and the absence of any such relation in that of Aquinas, between the sin and the suffering. In characterising the physical anguish of hell, Aquinas deliberately and dispassionately applies all his lucid force of statement to explaining how horrible it is. The physical suffering of Christ upon the cross exceeded anything that any man on earth ever had or ever has suffered. But the pains both of purgatory and of hell exceed it, and the pains of hell are never-ending. But there is no other relation between the sinful preference and the punishment than that the one is inflicted on account of the other. The punishment is imposed upon the sinner by the sentence of a court simply on the ground that he deserves to be pun-

ished. Whereas almost every reader of Dante's *Inferno*, unless he is merely revolted or paralysed by a sense of horror, feels, vaguely at first perhaps, but with growing clearness and deepening awe as he finds his way to the heart of the poem, that whereas others have said and say, "By the justice of God the sinner gets what he *deserves*," Dante sees exactly what the sinner *chose*, and conceives of the Divine justice as giving him that.

Thus as Dante passes with Virgil by the morass in which the passionate are tearing each other, he sees bubbles rising and breaking upon the surface. His guide tells him that they rise from the throats of the sullen souls that lie in the mud at the bottom of the morass. They cry: "Dismal we were in the sweet air, which the sun gladdens, nursing in our hearts the sullen fumes. Now we are dismal in this black mud." That is what sulking is. It is a deliberate and sustained effort to shut out the light and air of human fellowship, friendship, affection, and comfort, and to nurse sullen fumes in the heart, in the hope that this conduct may hurt others. "Dismal we were in the sweet air which the sun makes glad, nursing in our hearts the sullen fumes." That is what the sulky chose. To be in hell they have only to get it.

We must not try to push this principle that the punishment is simply the sin itself into every detail. The mistake is sometimes made. But you cannot compress the vision of a great poet into a single mechanical formula. Nevertheless, it is true that the atmosphere of Dante's hell is pervaded by this sense of congruousness between the fate of the sinners and their choice. A quite simple student of Dante once said to me, with a kind of bewilderment, speaking of the souls in hell, "But they don't seem to *want* to get out." It is true. Tortured and often resentful as they are, they are in a sense in a congenial atmosphere. The choice that brought them to hell and that finds its fitting environment there, is essentially their choice still. They are at home and in their own place in hell. In no true and integral sense do they "want to get out." It is this that gives its awful and august impersonality to Dante's hell. He speaks from time to time of the divine vengeance, it is true, but what he makes us feel is not the vengeance of God, but the shame of that evil choice that makes a self-wrought hell for man,—and the infinite "pity of it."

Nothing can redeem the conception of an eternal hell shared alike by Aquinas and Dante, nor suppress our protest against the Christian Church having added to all the mysteries of the universe that we cannot escape the gratuitous horror of this dogma. But granted that neither of these great minds could escape it, the contrast between their treatments of it remains. It is true that Aquinas is very seldom thinking or writing about hell, for it occupies but a very minute fraction of his work; whereas Dante devotes one-third of his great poem to it. But Dante's treatment illuminates the whole subject of the evil choice, burning and freezing into our hearts the sense of the nature and meaning of sin itself. Whereas Aquinas only insists on the awfulness of its consequences. But above all, Dante does not explain hell, though he informs it with a solemn meaning. Aquinas

does not make it mean anything; but he explains it as included in the act by which God wills his own goodness. And so Aquinas seems to carry hell into the very heart of our conception of the Divine Goodness, and the thought haunts us wherever we go in the vast and beautiful regions of his mind, until at last we deal with his explanation in the way in which he himself refuses to deal with hell—we come to think of its presence in his mind as a mystery, we refuse to take it with us, and so at last we come to feel the tenderness of his piety and the beauty of his spiritual insight in spite of our knowing all the time that there is something in his mind which we cannot explain, and which, if we thought of it, would baffle and perplex our souls and smirch the beauty of the mind with which we are conversing. That beauty is real. The presence of that other thought in its midst, is a mystery, and we forget it.

Now this is just what Dante seems to do with hell itself. Since he has not explained it, we can treat it as a mystery. In the ineffable Presence we forget it, but we carry with us the insight we gained as we put the spirits to question "in the deepest pool of the universe." And when the *thought* of hell is drowned in the light of heaven, the transfigured *experience* of hell is absorbed into it.

Francis Fergusson

The Metaphor of the Journey

For the first line of the first canto of the *Divine Comedy* Dante wrote:

Nel mezzo del cammin di nostra vita

(In the middle of the journey of our life)

There everything starts: in the middle of human life considered as a journey. There Dante was so lost and terrified that the journey to the realms beyond the grave became necessary for his salvation. But there too he found the strength and vision he required.

Dante knew that "the journey of our life" was a metaphor. He knew that the journey beyond the grave was a vastly extended metaphor also, in its literal meaning a fiction. But it was the miraculously right metaphor for his purposes, for what he had to show were the swarming journeys of human life with a clarity, vital intensity, and hidden order which seem to be indeed that of death, the aspect of eternity.

Knowing the fictiveness of his poem, knowing its sources, its manifold techniques, and all the subtle stratagems of its make-believe, he certainly did not believe it literally. But he believed, beyond our capacity for belief, in the truth which his fiction was devised to show. He tells Can Grande that his purpose was "to remove those living in this life from the state of misery, and lead them to the state of felicity." He reveals the truth of the human condition: the state of misery in the beginning of the poem, the state of felicity, after so many changing scenes, at the end. He does not preach: the journey speaks for

him. But the journey has a double movement, the literal narrative and the movement of understanding, which is always going from the make-believe of the visionary scene to the truth beneath it: to the human spirit, on its way, or milling in some deathly eddy.

The notion of human life as a journey, and the related notion that the guides of the race must journey beyond the grave and meet the spirits of the ancestors in order to grasp their earthly way and ours, seems to be as old as the myth-making instinct itself. Dante likens his mission to the legendary missions of Aeneas and Paul, both of whom had to acquire the second, the post-mortem vision. Behind the legends of Aeneas's and Paul's journeys to the other world lie the myths of prehistoric culture-heroes, which were associated with *rites de passage,* ceremonies of initiation marking the stages of human life from the cradle to the grave. The *Divine Comedy* may be regarded as an initiation, or series of initiations, into the wisdom of the tribe. But Dante's tribe had an old and complex civilization, and Dante is not merely primitive. He is, at the same time, at least as sophisticated in his own way as the hero of a modern *Bildungsroman:* Hans Castorp, say, doing his reading in his mountain sanitarium, or one of Henry James's American pilgrims, undergoing his initiation on the "stage of Europe."

In the countless uses which Dante makes of metaphors of journeying, he never loses the primitive power of the metaphor, yet at the same time he employs it for the sub-

From F. Fergusson, *Dante's Drama of the Mind*, Princeton University Press, 1953; reprinted by permission of the publishers.

tlest metaphysical and epistemological distinctions. All the journey-metaphors are based on the analogy, which the human mind finds very natural, between physical movement and the non-spatial action of the soul. The direct force of this analogy is unmistakable (for example) in Ulysses' narrative of his last ocean-voyage, in *Inferno*, Canto XXVI. But Ulysses' journey is in a carefully-controlled relation of analogy to Dante's journey down into Hell. It is also analogous to his subsequent journey up the Mount of Purgatory; but the journey into Hell is not continuous with the journey of purgation. The Pilgrim's transition from the one to the other is left mysterious, and each has its own validity as a metaphor for one aspect of earthly life. I have already mentioned the distinction between any of the journeys beyond the grave and the journey of this life. There are also the journeys of the making of the canticles, which are likened to sea-voyages, though *different* sea-voyages, in the opening sequences of the *Purgatorio* and the *Paradiso*. The reader too is supposed to be making a journey, at his peril, under Dante's guidance (*Paradiso*, Canto II, line 1):

> O voi, che siete in piccioletta barca,
>   desiderosi d'ascoltar, seguiti
>   retro al mio legno che cantando varca,
> tornate a riveder li vostri liti:
>   non vi mettete in pelago; chè forse,
>   perdendo me, rimarreste smarriti.

> (O you, who are there in your little boat,
>   longing to listen, following my way
>   behind my timbers singing as they go,
> turn you back to find your own coasts again:
>   do not trust to the open sea; for perhaps,
>   once losing me, you would be left astray.)

As one gets used to reading the *Divine Comedy*, one learns to see that Dante is continually correcting and amplifying one metaphorical journey with another; and by that means creating a sense of ceaseless life and movement, and of perpetually deepening, yet more and more closely-defined meaning.

II

One can see in a general way why Dante should have had to descend to the bottom of Hell before the other journeys became possible. Once in the terror of the Dark Wood, he had to explore the full import of that experience before his spirit was free to take another direction. And the vision of Hell is the occasion, the necessary preliminary to the other visions. Hell is the death which must precede rebirth, a moment which recurs by analogy through the whole poem: a moment in that tragic rhythm which governs the movement of the *Divine Comedy* in the whole and in its parts.

After the release from Hell, the incommensurable journey of purgation can get under way; but we know that it does not reach the final Goal which Dante envisaged. The *Paradiso*, another journey altogether, unfolds Divinity as reflected in the order of the Dantesque cosmos. The beatific vision may be regarded as the center of the whole *Commedia*, because in Dante's living belief God is the clue to all our modes of life, including the life and form of his poem. Dante regarded himself as the heir of Aeneas and Paul; he certainly believed that he both saw and wrote in obedience to God. Yet at the same time he had a disabused and tender sense of mortal limitations, his own and the reader's; and he placed the vision of God outside the poem —an End and a Center which must remain ineffable. He explains clearly to Can Grande that he does not intend to explore heaven as the theologians try to do, speculatively, as it would be in itself. He reflects it, in successive aspects, in a changing human spirit, and only as it avails for the actual life—the nourishment and guidance— of that spirit. And the *Paradiso* also is based upon the journey-metaphor.

"But the *branch of philosophy* which regulates the work in its whole and in its parts," says Dante, explaining the *Comedy* to Can Grande, "is morals or ethics, because the whole was undertaken not for speculation but for practical results." Ethics and morals, and all didacticism, are in bad odor with us because we do not have much faith in our moralists. But when Dante says "moral philosophy" he means something like the natural history of the human psyche, the accumulated lore of its life. And when he says that this "philosophy" regulates the whole poem, including the *Paradiso*, he means that the underlying subject is always the modes of being and the destiny of the human psyche. The *Paradiso* presents it in relation to many reflections of its transcendent end; but it is the *Purgatorio* which explores the psyche itself —not in terms of its supernatural Goal, but in terms of its earthly existence.

It is therefore possible to read the *Purgatorio* both as a center of the whole *Commedia*, and as a poem with its own self-subsistent unity. The journey has its beginning in the *Antipurgatorio*, its center and turning-point in the evening of the second Day, its end in the *Paradiso Terrestre*. It is the visionary Fulfillment of the journey of *this* life, moving always, in many figures, toward what the soul may know of itself within its earthly destiny. It reflects Dante's own life, and by analogy, every man's.

The action of the *Purgatorio* has a natural source which is not too difficult to identify in one's own experience. After some deep fright, some nightmare-intuition of being nowhere, hope returns, and with hope the disquieting naïveté of the bare forked animal who needs to know who he is, where he is, and what he is trying to do. This need is, apparently, always with us. We may hear it in much of the murmuring of our innumerable radios, in popular music, in the vague complaining of the interminable soap-operas. We may detect it in ourselves whenever we are not too busy, sophisticated, or demoralized. The *Purgatorio* starts, after Hell, with this need; but Dante knew more about it than we do, and he found, in his time and place, the means to follow its promptings to the end.

Professor Maritain has spoken of the in-

nocence and luck of Dante. The innocence —inseparable from courage, and deep to the point of genius—underlies both the terror and the triumphs of his journeys. His luck has to do with the moment of history in which he worked. Dante's Europe, Christian but full of ancient, Arabic, and Hebrew influences, must have seemed divided, deceptive, and confusing to those who lived in it. There were plenty of wars (to make us feel at home); poets in pursuit of their heretical inspirations; rulers making absolute claims; dissentions foreign and domestic. Dante himself was a displaced person, and he had plenty of reason to see the journeys of this life as lost, caught in the dead-ends of Hell. And yet, as Professor Curtius has recently shown, the culture formed then was to continue proliferating into the Renaissance and far beyond it. Some of its themes may still be heard well into the eighteenth century. The *Divine Comedy* reflects the path which Dante discovered through the actual confusion about him to the vision of an ideal order: it may be regarded as the epic of the discovery of Europe's traditional culture. This is especially true of the *Purgatorio*, the transitional canticle, the poem of initiations. Shelley's description of the *Commedia* as a bridge across time, joining the ancient and the modern world, fits the *Purgatorio* exactly. Or Eliot's dictum: "Dante and Shakespeare divide the modern world between them; there is no third."

It is strange that the *Divine Comedy* should have begun to be read again, after its eclipse during the period of the Enlightenment, just when the disappearance of the traditional culture was first sharply felt— with the revolutionary movements of the early romantics. Perhaps that is because the need for a way of life can only be felt with a depth comparable to Dante's, when no common way of life exists.

III

Dante has plainly indicated the main stages of the purgatorial journey, in the chronology of the ascent of the Mountain, and in the varied scenes of the climb. The first Day is spent in the foothills of the *Antipurgatorio*. The first night marks the mysterious transition to the realm of purgation proper, within the Gates. The second Day shows the ascent of the Mountain, painfully, under Virgil's guidance; and the second night marks another important change. During the third Day the ascent is easier, the scene of the climb more rich and exhilarating. The third night is spent on the threshold of Eden, and during the morning of the fourth Day, Eden, the *Paradiso Terrestre*, is explored. The literal narrative is clear; it recounts the ascent of a Mountain, from its rugged foothills to the meadowy plateau on its summit. But the distance figured in this climb is not spatial, but spiritual, like that between childhood and age. The movement which the reader is supposed to follow is double: that of the literal climb, and a movement of understanding, to which the developing inner life of Dante the Pilgrim is the clue.

One may start to enjoy the poetry of the *Purgatorio* immediately, but there is no short cut to understanding, no possibility of looking up the answers at the back of the book. It is true that Dante used many maps and blue-prints in building his great theater for this journey. There is a geographical plan, and an astronomical scheme governing the significant and elaborately worked-out chronology. There is a moral map, a Thomistic-Aristotelian classification of sins, with Pride at the bottom, nearest to Hell, and Lust at the top, nearest to Eden. The commentators have worked out most of these blueprints clearly, and their results are summarized in the excellent notes and appendices of the Temple Classics edition. But these abstract schemes have no more to do with what goes on in the poem than a road-map has to do with hitch-hiking to Chicago. Dante did not believe that the varied modes of human life could be "known" abstractly; the knowledge he seeks to convey is so close to home

that it may actually avail to free and nourish the spirit. That is why, instead of writing a psychology, he dramatizes the acquisition of insight, carefully distinguishing between what he knows as author of the poem and what it takes, and means, to get knowledge.

Dante writes the poem as the record of a journey which he once took and now remembers. He writes in the first person; and yet the distinction between Dante speaking as the author, and Dante the Pilgrim, is fundamental to the whole structure. The author, when he reminds us of his existence, is outside the fictive world of the poem; the Pilgrim is the protagonist of the drama, the center of each scene. The author knows the whole story in advance, the Pilgrim meets everything freshly, for the first time. The two perspectives together produce a sort of stereoptical effect, that of an objective and partially mysterious reality. The shifting tensions between the two make the complex movement of the poem, and sustain its suspense. The Pilgrim is very much like one of Henry James's central intelligences, visible himself as a particular individual, yet revealing to the reader both the story and its meaning as he learns it. The Pilgrim's awareness is always moving toward the author's, but when they coincide, in the very strange and wonderful close of the *Paradiso Terrestre*, all narrative movement, and all growth of understanding, cease. While the poem unfolds, the Pilgrim's awareness is the moving center of the composition.

Dante explained to Can Grande how his poem was to be read and understood. "The exposition of the letter," he wrote, "is nought else than the development of the form." By the *letter* he meant the literal fiction of the journeys to the other world, all that the Pilgrim sees and feels and hears there. By the *development of the form* he meant that musical or dramatic unfolding which I tried to describe above: the drama of the Pilgrim's growing understanding. It has not, I think, been sufficiently noticed how strongly Dante puts his prescription for interpreting his poem: the exposition (or interpretation) *is* the development of the form—not any aspect of the structure which may be abstracted and considered as a static scheme, but the shifting life of the growing soul itself, imitated in the ceaseless movement of the *terza rima*.

The plan of these studies is intended to follow Dante's prescription as I understand it. Each phase of the journey—from childhood to age, or from innocence to natural sanctity—has its own irreducible significance, its own mode of understanding, which is imitated in the poem itself. The four parts of the book are devoted to the four Days of the journey. The titles I have used for the four Days are intended to suggest the nature of the drama, always a struggle for freedom and understanding, but going on in a different way in each phase of growth. It is necessary to linger over each one, because they are so different from each other.

IV

Dante announces the theme of the whole *Purgatorio,* with his usual decision, in the opening chords of the very first canto:

Per correr miglior acqua alza le vele
   omai la navicella del mio ingegno,
   che lascia retro a sè mar sì crudele.

(To run over better waters now hoists sail
   the little bark of my native talent,
   which leaves behind it a sea so cruel.)

The search for the better describes the action, the movement-of-spirit, of the whole poem. But the metaphor of the ocean-voyage is not connected with the journey up the Mountain. Dante is speaking as author, outside the fictive world of the *Purgatorio,* of a journey which is neither that of this life, nor that of Hell, but the hope-inspired journey of the *making* of this canticle:

E canterò di quel secondo regno
   dove l'umano spirito si purga,
   e di salire al ciel diventa degno.

(And I shall sing of that second kingdom
   wherein the human spirit is made clean,
   becoming worthy to ascend to heaven.)

He goes on (lines 7–13) to bid dead poetry, the poetry of the ancient world, to rise again to help him.

We feel the lift of the ocean-voyage through the whole passage, as we do in the more triumphant use of that metaphor in the second canto of the *Paradiso,* which I quoted above. We may also remember the ocean-music of Ulysses' superb narrative of his foolish flight into these realms (Inferno XXVI)—"to seek virtue and knowledge," as he told his followers. This is one of several echoes of Ulysses' voyage in the first canto, and no doubt Dante wishes to suggest an analogy between Ulysses' motive and the aspiration which moves him to poetry here. But he does not offer explanations of these relationships. We know that the Pilgrim, leaving Ulysses, descended to the bottom, and then found that his descent had mysteriously turned into a climb upward. We know that Ulysses was wrecked on a Mountain which he had not foreseen. The aspiration of this canticle is like Ulysses' but reborn beyond his confines. But it would be a mistake to try to connect these voyages literally: they are different, and very Dantesque, uses of the journey-metaphor, each with its own relation to the journey of this life.

In line 13 we suddenly find ourselves in this realm, at the beginning of this journey, with the Pilgrim, weak after Hell, where dawn finds him on the beach:

Dolce color d'oriental zaffiro,
   che s'accoglieva nel sereno aspetto
   dell'aer puro infino al primo giro,
agli occhi miei ricominciò diletto,
   tosto ch'i'uscii fuor dell'aura morta,
   che m'avea contristati gli occhi e il petto.

(The tender color of the eastern sapphire,
   which was appearing in the tranquil height
   of pure air, as far as the first gyre,
restored to my eyes once more their delight,
   as soon as I emerged from the dead air
   which had so saddened both my eyes and heart.)

The author, outside the poem, speaks with a sense of its vast scope, its difference from life itself, and its varied but related themes of journeying. But the Pilgrim can only see the comforting return of an earthly dawn. The distance between them suggests the distance we have to go, and the childlike state of being with which *this* journey begins.

Charles S. Singleton

The Pattern at the Center

THE triumphal procession which comes in the forest at the top of the mountain of Purgatory is the triumph of Beatrice. This is known to us—or ought to be—once we have read the poem. But it is something we must *unknow* for purposes of reading the poem even a second time, if we are to find there, in the coming of Beatrice, that special kind of meaning which only an art form can give: a meaning emerging out of the unfolding of a particular form and from that process inseparable, indeed non-existent. For, as the poem would have it, we come to Beatrice by a quite special way. And when we see her, finally, she stands framed in a meaning that is created and established by the very path of our approach. To point to this, of course, is to point to nothing new in poetry; but precisely to that kind of meaning with which students of literature as an art are first of all concerned—or ought to be.

The way to Beatrice in the poem is built along the line of a reader's expectation, an expectation which is planted in us by the words Virgil speaks to his charge in dismissing him at the edge of the garden:

> Vedi lo sol che in fronte ti riluce;
>   vedi l'erbetta, i fiori e li arbuscelli,
>   che qui la terra sol da sé produce.
> Mentre che vegnan lieti li occhi belli
>   che, lacrimando, a te venir mi fenno,
>   seder ti puoi e puoi andar tra elli.
> *Purgatorio* XXVII, 133–138.

See the sun shining upon your face; see the grass, the flowers and the shrubs which here the earth produces by itself alone. While the beautiful eyes are coming in gladness which, in tears, caused me to come to you, you may sit among these things and you may go.

This can only be Beatrice who is expected. This is indeed only a reminder of what from the beginning we have known would come to pass when we reached this point in the journey.

As we move into the garden we come to a stream. Suddenly, in a meadow there beyond the stream, we see a maiden gathering flowers and singing as she goes. And we wonder: can this be Beatrice? No, it cannot be, for Dante does not appear to recognize her. This (we learn her name later) is Matelda. Dante may not yet cross the river and possess her, as he so much desires to do at once. But where is Beatrice? We were expecting her to come.

The stream along which we walked turns, so that in following it we face the east. Suddenly, throughout the forest there is a flash of light like lightning, and with it a sweet melody. And the poet breaks off his narrative to call upon all nine of the muses now for aid that he may set down in verses things hard to grasp in thought.

Is this Beatrice who is coming? Someone, surely, is coming; and coming as in some triumphal entry, for the melody, as it draws nearer, proves to be voices chanting and in the chant we make out the cry *Hosanna*.

Now with measured step a procession comes into view. It is one hard indeed to set down in prose, much less in verse, so is it laden with symbolic suggestion in all its

Reprinted by permission of the publishers from Charles S. Singleton, *Dante Studies I—Commedia: Elements of Structure*, Cambridge, Mass., Harvard University Press, copyright 1954 by the President and Fellows of Harvard College.

detail. The poet, in the verses, brings it into view only gradually. We see the parts of it, one after another, in the strict order of their emerging. But, to get it before our mind's eye again, we may review this procession as it is displayed to our view *after* it has wholly emerged and come to a halt before us.

At the head of the whole, as it came forward, were seven lights or lamps, advancing as by miracle, since no bearers of these are visible. These lamps have left back over the whole procession seven bands or streamers of light which will continue to hang over it all the while, like a kind of heaven. Next, following the lamps, come twenty-four figures called elders (*seniori*), robed in white and distinct, as a first group in the procession, by virtue of the crowns of lilies which they wear. Next, following this first group and (as we come to see), at the center of the whole, come four strange wingèd animals, crowned in green. These, as they come, contain in the square of space between them another strange animal, half eagle and half lion, a gryphon, hitched to a two-wheeled chariot which it draws after it and at the wheels of which seven maidens are dancing. This central group is then followed by yet a third, made up of nine figures dressed in white like the first group of elders, but these with crowns of red.

This, of course, is to distinguish rapidly only the principal parts and more salient features of the procession as it halts there across the river. As we watched it (in the poem) come into view, a profusion of symbolic detail of color and gesture has helped us to see the parts for what they are and finally the whole for what it is. And we may safely assign names to the parts and to the whole.

The seven lights heading the procession and hanging back over it as a bright canopy are (in figure) the sevenfold gift of the Holy Spirit, the Spirit which presided over the writing of Holy Scripture and (for reasons we shall see) the same Spirit which

the prophet Isaiah foretold would descend upon the Christ who was to come.[1] The procession, then, that follows the lights is unmistakably a procession of Holy Scripture itself. Here come now, not the authors of the books of Holy Scripture, but the books themselves and in the number and order in which they are (or were) known. First, all the books of the Old Testament, twenty-four of them, crowned in white, the color of faith. Next the four gospels, figured in the four strange animals, crowned in their turn in the color of hope. And last, as a third group, the remaining books of the New Testament crowned in the color of charity. In the figure bringing up the rear, we recognize Revelation.

But clearly more than the books of Scripture have a part in this procession. For at its center, contained by the four gospels, is a gryphon which, in its dual nature, figures Christ; and a chariot which is His Church. The seven maidens dancing at the wheels, four on one side and three on the other, are the moral and the theological virtues.

It is the chariot that marks the center of the whole procession. For one thing, when, at a signal like thunder, the whole comes to a halt, it is the chariot which is directly across the river from Dante—Dante who is and who remains our post of observation. Moreover, upon the halt of the whole parade, the elders who came ahead of the gryphon and His chariot, turn to face the chariot so that, in a quite literal sense, all eyes are upon the vehicle at the center.

But, now that we have the procession before us in its whole length and framed in this way, it is well to recall again that the

[1] Isaiah 11, 2: "Et requiescet super eum spiritus Domini: spiritus sapientiae et intellectus, spiritus consilii et fortitudinis, spiritus scientiae et pietatis; et replebit eum spiritus timoris Domini." *Cf. Convivio* IV, xxi, 11 ff.

The point of importance is that, by way of the prophetic nature of the passage in Isaiah and its vision *of the Christ to come*, we have in this feature of the procession (and at the very beginning) the kind of signal which can coöperate with the others in this respect.

poet does not give it to us so. On the contrary, he brings it into view in the manner of an emerging. We see successive parts only as these can be discerned from where Dante stands, gradually, one after the other, and in due order. The form here matters. For if this is Holy Scripture that comes here (and we know that it is), if this is the Word of God that comes so, we see that the poet has so managed the coming of that Word as to give us the distinct impression that it has unfolded before our eyes, that Scripture has come into view in the due order of its books, from the beginning to Revelation. By the form, by this process of unfolding, a dimension of meaning is put here that we must not miss. For, if this is the Word of God gradually emerging, where else could that take place if not in time? By such a form it is precisely *time* which is put here. And thereby is framed an aspect of symbolic significance which, I think, we may be helped to see by an observation on Holy Scripture which St. Bonaventura makes in the prologue to his *Breviloquium:*

Holy Scripture has a length which consists of the description of the times and ages, namely, from the beginning of the world to the day of judgment. . . . Thus Scripture is of great length, because in its treatment it begins with the commencement of the world and of time, in the beginning of Genesis—and extends to the end of the world and of time, to the end of the Apocalypse.[2]

Bonaventura, we may be sure, was not the first to see in the length of Scripture this symbolic meaning. It is a meaning in symbol firmly enough established that a Christian poet can build with it.

It is at just the moment when the whole

procession has fully emerged and halted before us that we can best feel the impact of the symbolic meaning. This, literally, is Holy Scripture coming in time. And now that it is all there before us, we have Scripture there as we, who come after its coming in time, do have it. This now is Scripture in that kind of timeless dimension in which it stands as it is spread in this life before the eyes of every faithful Christian. But St. Bonaventura has helped us to see more here, to see a figure of time itself unfolding from its beginning to its end. So now, how is it with time when the procession halts? Has time itself, in some way, come to a standstill? If so, then the pattern itself, in its symbolic dimension, is signifying something, is making a call which we should hear. It is signaling something. Must that not be this: that a day of Judgment is at hand?

Standing back thus and viewing the pattern of the whole, we do see that we have here, in figure, a conception of time, of history, that could not be more Christian.[3] First of all, time here has a beginning and an end. And, as time unfolds from its beginning to its end, there at the center is Christ and His Church. And now time is unfolded, time is come to a halt, time is immobilized, with all eyes on the center, and something, someone, expected there. In this most Christian pattern, will that not be one who comes to judge? And who could that be, if not Christ Himself? The very

---

[2] *Opera omnia* (Quaracchi, 1891) Tome V, p. 203: "De longitudine sacrae Scripturae." *See also* at the end of this chapter: "Et quia nullus homo tam longaevus est quod totam possit videre oculis carnis suae, nec futura potest per se praevidere; providit nobis Spiritus Sanctus librum Scripturae sacrae, cuius longitudo commetitur se decursui regiminis universi."

[3] On the essential features of such a Christian conception of history a number of important studies may be consulted: O. Cullman, *Christ and Time,* trans. Filson (Philadelphia, 1950); R. Niebuhr, *Faith and History* (New York, 1949); E. C. Rust, *The Christian Understanding of History* (London, 1947); P. Tillich, *The Interpretation of History,* trans. Rasetzki and Talmey (New York, 1936); and the important article by J. Daniélou, "The Problem of Symbolism," in *Thought* XXV (1950), 423 ff. Also the brief but most illuminating essay by E. Frank, "St. Augustine and Greek Thought" (Cambridge, Mass., The Augustinian Society, 1942), p. 11: "The Epiphany of Christ was the center of his [Augustine's] historical speculation."

pattern of the procession before us seems now to be calling for Him to come.

In yet another way we can see that the scene before us is making a most urgent call for something, for someone, to come there at the center. For the chariot there, we must not forget, is a triumphal chariot. Rome, the poem tells us, had no finer for its Caesar. It is a remarkable vehicle. And yet, surely, not the least remarkable thing about it is this: it is empty. There is no one in triumph on this triumphal chariot; and since there is no one there, surely someone is expected there. The elders have turned and faced it. All eyes that came before it and all that came after it are now upon it. Is Christ to appear upon it? But is not Christ given here in the procession by the gryphon who pulls the chariot? And were we not expecting Beatrice?

We go back thus to that expectation as to a thread that can guide us through all this by revealing to us, as we move along it, the certain outline of a poet's intention. We expect Beatrice. But all the while everything, the pattern of the whole, the image of time immobilized and expectant at its center, all seems to call for Christ.

It is indeed time to go back and remember that this thread of an intention becomes especially clear as the procession unfolds, for as it advances we hear utterances, cries and shouts that are an unmistakable part of that intention. First, as the chanting came nearer, it was the cry *Hosanna* that we heard. Then, as they came forward with their eyes upon the guiding spirit of the Lord, the books of the Old Testament —those forward-looking and prophetic books—shouted in unison what is surely the salutation of Gabriel to Mary: "Benedicta tue nelle figlie d'Adamo."

Can those words be heralding anything if not the Christ who is to come? But as we came into this garden, we had been given to expect Beatrice. Indeed, when the procession halts and those elders have turned about to face the empty chariot, one of them (unmistakably the Song of Solo-

mon) utters another welcoming cry which would seem to call now for some lady to come. Thrice he shouts "Veni sponsa de Libano" and clearly the spectator (and reader) is expected to hear the word which follows upon that utterance in the Canticle itself and completes it: *Corona-beris* ("thou shalt be crowned").

> Tota pulchra es, amica mea,
> et macula non est in te.
> Veni de Libano, sponsa mea,
> veni de Libano, veni, *coronaberis.*[4]

Then finally, when all is halted, and when all eyes are upon the empty chariot, we see appear upon it, first, many angels who arise with a welcoming cry, calling in their turn now for the one who is to come. And their shout is: *Benedictus qui venis*. The poet could have had it "Benedicta quae venis" without the slightest metrical difficulty. But no, the cry is Benedic*tus*. Surely a poet could not more clearly reveal his guiding intention.

Moreover the very image by which Beatrice does, at long last, come to stand upon the chariot is the final seal upon this intention. For the figure by which she appears is that of the sun rising behind morning mists. We may note first of all, of course, the accuracy of the image with respect to the immediate situation. We remember that we are still facing the east, that it is early morning in the garden. Then, on the chariot, there arise figures, tossing flowers so as to make a veritable cloud of these. And within, or rather through, that cloud Beatrice appears. The image is accurate. But it is designed to be more than that, to fulfill a larger purpose and pattern, and this we are now in a better position to see. For we must know that the image of a rising sun could bring with it, out of a long traditional usage, an established burden of symbolic meaning. A rising sun was the image for Christ, the established image for the com-

---

[4] Canticum Canticorum 4, 8. The King James Version does not translate the "coronaberis," so important for our considerations.

ing of Christ.[5] Later, in Paradise, we may even see the confirmation of this. For there, where Christ comes in what is truly His triumph, He comes as a sun.[6] And here now, at the center, where the very configuration of the procession itself has seemed to call for Him, here now, as angels strew a cloud of flowers in the air and shout *Benedictus qui venis,* here Beatrice is at last given to us by the very image which, for so long before, had given Christ in His coming:

> Io vidi già nel cominciar del giorno
> la parte oriental tutta rosata,
> e l'altro ciel di bel sereno adorno;
> e la faccia del sol nascere ombrata,
> sì che, per temperanza di vapori,
> l'occhio la sostenea lunga fiata:
> così dentro una nuvola di fiori
> che da le mani angeliche saliva
> e ricadeva in giù dentro e di fori,
> sovra candido vel cinta d'uliva
> donna m'apparve . . .
>
> *Purgatorio* XXX, 22–32.

At times I have seen, at the start of day, the east all rosy and the rest of the sky adorned with beautiful serenity; and the face of the sun rise overcast, so that, through its being tempered by mists, the eye could endure it a long while.

So, within a cloud of flowers rising from angels' hands and falling again within and without, crowned with olive over a white veil, dressed in the color of living flame beneath a cloak of green, a lady appeared to me. . . .

At last there is someone in triumph upon the chariot at the center. What in so many ways was called for is now delivered. A pattern is fulfilled. It is not Christ who comes. It is Beatrice—Beatrice who comes *as* Christ.

But we have yet to observe here an even more striking point of detail. The pattern before us, as we saw, was not signaling merely *a* coming of Christ. But, because the procession of Scripture could symbol-

ize time itself; and, as it came to a halt, could suggest time at an end; because we could feel that now we had before us somehow time at a standstill, with all eyes on the center, we could sense the signal (this being the Christian pattern of time that it is) that a day of Judgment might be at hand.

Is this particular of the pattern fulfilled? Is this signal of a day of Judgment met and answered when Beatrice does come? Yes, even this. We get, in a simile, the first confirmation of it. For, as the angels rise up on the chariot, scattering their cloud of flowers and shouting their cry of welcome (*Benedictus qui venis*), the manner of their rising there is said to be as that of the saints shall be on the day of the Resurrection:

> Quali i beati al novissimo bando
> surgeran presti ognun di sua caverna,
> la revestita carne alleluiando;
> cotali in su la divina basterna
> si levar cento, ad vocem tanti senis,
> ministri e messaggier di vita etterna.
> Tutti dicean: *"Benedictus qui venis!"*
>
> *Purgatorio* XXX, 13–19.

As the blessed at the last trumpet will arise quickly each from his tomb, praising the Lord for the resurrected flesh; so at the voice of such an elder did a hundred ministers and messengers of life eternal arise upon the divine chariot. All were saying: *"Benedictus qui venis!"*

It is a figure almost too transparent in the way it reveals a poet's intention. There may be no mistake about it. The coming of Beatrice has completely fulfilled the demands of the pattern. As Christ will come at His second coming, so does Beatrice come here: in a cloud of glory, at the end of time and at the center of time—to judge. The analogue is complete.

For we soon see that Beatrice has come to judge, to stand in sternest judgment on one whose name is the first word she utters: Dante.

And we hear from her now the reproach-

---

[5] On the Sun image in this respect, *see* especially H. F. Dunbar, *Symbolism in Medieval Thought,* etc. (New Haven, 1929), pp. 105 ff. and *passim.*
[6] *Paradiso* XXIII, 29.

es by which we are reminded of the role she had had in the poet's life. Beatrice goes over the facts of the past, reads them out of the Book of Memory. (*Thou art worthy to take the book and open the seals thereof.*) [7] The *Comedy* here gathers into itself the experience of the *Vita Nuova*, may be said to build on to the earlier work. Among her reproaches we have, in a single terzina, the statement of the part she had played in Dante's life in her brief time on earth:

Alcun tempo il sostenni col mio volto:
    mostrando li occhi giovanetti a lui,
    meco il menava in dritta parte volto.
                                Purgatorio XXX, 121-123.

For a time I sustained him with my face: letting him see my young eyes, I guided him turned in the right direction.

By such a role she had deserved the name *salute* so often assigned to her in the *Vita Nuova*; indeed, had so earned her own true name, *Beatrice*. She had died. And now, ten years later, she comes from above and beyond to judge him, comes with a charge of the backsliding of which he is guilty in the years since her death:

Quando di carne a spirto era salita,
    e bellezza e virtù cresciuta m'era,
    fu'io a lui men cara e men gradita;
e volse i passi suoi per via non vera,
    imagini di ben seguendo false,
    che nulla promission rendono intera.
Nè l'impetrare ispirazion mi valse,
    con le quali ed in sogno e altrimenti
    lo rivocai; sì poco a lui ne calse!
Tanto giù cadde, che tutti argomenti
    a la salute sua eran già corti,
    fuor che mostrarli le perdute genti.
Per questo visitai l'uscio de'morti,
    e a colui che l'ha qua su condotto,
    li preghi miei, piangendo, furon porti.
                                Purgatorio XXX, 127-141.

When I had arisen from flesh to spirit, and my beauty and virtue had increased, I was less dear

to him and less cherished; and he turned his steps along an untrue way, following after false images of good which yield no promise to the full. Nor did obtaining inspirations avail me, with which both in dreams and otherwise I called him back: so little did he care about it! He fell so low that all measures for his salvation were by then insufficient except by showing him the lost people. Therefore I visited the gate of the dead, and, with tears, to him who has led him up here, my entreaties were taken.

Let this be observed first of all: the analogy of Beatrice to Christ, built up before our eyes in the last cantos of the *Purgatorio*, is no arbitrary, no ornamental, way devised by a poet to praise his lady. It is in Beatrice's role in Dante's life that that analogy finds its full and impressive support. We must hold the *Vita Nuova* and the *Comedy* together at this point (and this is something which the *Comedy* here invites us to do) if we are to see this. We know from the *Vita Nuova* how Beatrice had come into the poet's life as a miracle, as a love descending from Heaven to light an upward way to salvation.[8] And now we learn from her reproaches that, after her death, she had come again to him in visions to recall him to the supernal goal. We have known, too, from the beginning of the poem, what she recounts here: that for him she had descended to Hell, to Virgil in Limbo, to lay open the way to salvation. Analogy is not an equivalence. Analogy is a resemblance. Clearly these things do reflect other things: the coming of Another Love upon earth, the descent of Another to Hell, the coming of Another in visions after His death. But, now that we are holding the *Vita Nuova* and the *Comedy* together and reading the story which they together tell, I would point out one aspect of the whole analogy which seems till now to have escaped our notice—a most central aspect. An attentive

---

[7] Revelation 5, 8-9: "And when he had taken the book, the four beasts and the four and twenty elders fell down before the Lamb . . . and they sung a new song, saying, Thou art worthy . . . , etc."

[8] For a full discussion of this aspect of the *Vita Nuova* see the author's *Essay on the Vita Nuova*, especially Chapter III, "From Love to Caritas." *See also* for the analogy Beatrice-Christ and the pattern at the center in that work.

reader of the *Vita Nuova* of course knows
that the earlier work itself pointed up an
analogy Beatrice–Christ—did so, indeed,
so boldly that a later century, the sixteenth,
unable to understand that this was analogy,
expurgated the work in its first printed edition, deleting the closing words of Chapter
XXIV, for instance, where we read how
the poet one day had seen Beatrice coming
in the company of another gentle lady and
following after this lady as she came:

. . . io vidi venire verso me una gentile donna,
la quale era di famosa bieltade, e fue già molto
donna di questo primo mio amico. E lo nome di
questa donna era Giovanna, salvo che per la sua
bieltade, secondo che altri crede, imposto l'era
nome Primavera; e così era chiamata. E appresso lei, guardando, vidi venire la mirabile
Beatrice. Queste donne andaro presso di me così
l'una appresso l'altra, e parve che Amore mi par-
lasse nel cuore, e dicesse: "Quella prima è no-
minata Primavera solo per questa venuta d'oggi;
chè io mossi lo imponitore del nome a chiamarla
così Primavera, cioè prima verrà lo die che Beatrice si mosterrà dopo la imaginazione del suo
fedele. E se anche vogli considerare lo primo
nome suo, tanto è quanto dire 'prima verrà,'
però che lo suo nome Giovanna è da quello Giovanni lo quale precedette la verace luce, di-
cendo: 'Ego vox clamantis in deserto: parate
viam Domini.' "

Vita Nuova, Chapter XXIV.

I saw coming toward me a gentle lady who was
famous for her beauty and who had formerly
been very much the lady of this first friend of
mine. And the name of this lady was Joan except
that because of her beauty, as some believe, she
had been given the name Primavera; and so was
she called. These ladies passed near me thus
one after the other, and it seemed to me that
Love spoke to me in my heart and said: "She
who comes first is named Primavera for just this
her coming today; because I moved the giver of
the name to name her thus *Primavera*, that is,
prima verrà on that day when Beatrice will appear after the imagination of her faithful one.
And if you will also consider her first name, it is
tantamount to saying 'prima verrà' because her
name Joan is from that John who preceded the
True Light saying: *Ego vox clamantis in deserto; parate viam Domini.*"

Certainly the poet has not wanted us to
miss this analogy—one indeed already
manifest in the chapter immediately preceding this, the twenty-third (which could
thus hardly be nearer the center of the *Vita
Nuova*) a chapter where, in a vision which
came to him as he lay sick of a fever, the
death of Beatrice is announced to the poet
amid signs of universal cataclysm that can
only remind us of the death of Christ (and,
by yet other signs, of His Ascension):

Così cominciando ad errare la mia fantasia, ven-
ni a quello ch'io non sapea ove io mi fosse; e
vedere mi parea donne andare scapigliate pian-
gendo per via, maravigliosamente triste; e pareami vedere lo sole oscurare, sì che le stelle si
mostravano di colore ch'elle mi faceano giudicare
che piangessero; a pareami che li uccelli vo-
lando per l'aria cadessero morti, e che fossero
grandissimi terremuoti. E maravigliandomi in co-
tale fantasia, e paventando assai, imaginai alcuno
amico che mi venisse a dire: "Or non sai? la tua
mirabile donna è partita di questo secolo." Allora
cominciai a piangere molto pietosamente; e non
solamente piangea ne la imaginazione, ma piangea con li occhi, bagnandoli di vere lagrime.
Io imaginava di guardare verso lo cielo, e pareami, vedere moltitudine d'angeli li quali tornassero
in suso, ed aveano dinanzi da loro una nebuletta
bianchissima. A me parea che questi angeli can-
tassero gloriosamente, e le parole del loro canto
mi parea udire che fossero queste: *Osanna in excelsis.* . . .

Vita Nuova, Chapter XXIII.

Thus, as my phantasy began to wander, I came
to such a point that I did not know where I was:
and I seemed to see women going along a way,
weeping and disheveled, marvelously sad: and I
seemed to see the sun grow dark so that the stars
came out with a color that made me judge them
to be weeping; and it seemed to me that the birds
flying through the air fell and that there were
very great earthquakes. And marveling in such a
phantasy and being greatly afraid, I imagined
that some friend came to me and said: "But
don't you know? Your marvelous lady is gone
from this world." Then I began to weep most
piteously; . . . I imagined that I looked toward
Heaven and I seemed to see a host of angels that
were returning upwards and they had before
them a very white little cloud. It seemed to me

that these angels sang gloriously and the words of their song, I seemed to hear, were these: *Hosanna in excelsis.* . . .

Why we have not seen it before, I do not know. Here are the reproaches of Beatrice inviting us to hold the *Vita Nuova* and the *Divine Comedy* together. Now do we not see what may be seen only if we do this? In the *Vita Nuova,* at the center of *Vita Nuova,* Beatrice is seen to depart this life, uplifted in the company of a host of angels, in a cloud, and the cry that accompanies her is *Hosanna.* At the center of the *Divine Comedy,* Beatrice comes, Beatrice returns, in the company of a host of angels, in a cloud of glory, and in a company whose first cry is again *Hosanna.* But what is more striking than all of these details is this: Beatrice's death at the center of the *Vita Nuova* is like Christ's death. We have seen the signs—like Christ's death and like an ascension. And at the center of the *Comedy,* Beatrice's return, what is thus literally Beatrice's second coming, resembles not *a* coming of Christ, but the *second* coming of Christ—in a day of Judgment.

The *Comedy* is built on to the *Vita Nuova* more essentially than we have imagined; we have only to look at the pattern which the one work and the other bears at its center.

We have been speaking of the last cantos of the *Purgatorio* as the center of the *Comedy.* But in what sense is this so? Is not the middle of the *Purgatorio* the center—cantos 16, 17, 18, where the great questions of love and free will are discussed? Yes, if we count the cantos. But if we will look, not at the surface symmetry of the poem, but somewhat deeper; if we will but consider the whole as an action, we shall see that at either end of that action, we are outside of time. Hell is beyond time, an eternal place. So too, of course, is the last heaven of light where God is. But from the first canto of *Purgatory* up to the Empyrean, in that area, that is, of the action that lies between these two eternal poles and

timeless *termini,* we are in time, we move in time. Just so much of this upward way to God is through time. And now we see that when Beatrice comes, she comes at the center of this stretch in time. It is as if the procession at the center, in so far as that could suggest in its unfolding the whole extent of time, had also held out the symbol of this. For, there, in a stretch of time so signified, Beatrice comes at the center. And so too in the upward action of the poem. Let there be a vertical line, a line of ascent in time in the upward way to God. And let there be a horizontal line, as it were, drawn across this vertical line by a procession symbolizing time. Where these lines meet, where these lines cross in the poem—there Beatrice comes—as Christ.[9]

Holding before us now what has been observed and standing back somewhat from the *Comedy,* we must see in this pattern at the center of the larger work certainly more than simply the continuation of an analogy Beatrice–Christ already built into the structure of the *Vita Nuova.* I would not exclaim here over another little symmetry of pattern or another rare correspondence of detail in Dante's work. We have to do here with something as profoundly essential as it is central.

What this is I may only briefly suggest. Clearly, we have here yet another manifestation of what we already had had glimpses of as the guiding principle of construction for this most Christian of poets. Before now we have recognized that with

[9] *Cf.* P. Tillich, *The Protestant Era,* trans. Adams (Chicago, 1948), p. 19: "This became obvious in the last creation of original Greek thought, Neo-Platonism, in which the horizontal line is entirely negated by the vertical one, and society is entirely devaluated for the sake of the individual soul. The emanation of the different degrees of reality from the ultimate One to mere matter and the return of the soul through the different spheres from matter to the ultimate One stabilize a vertical direction of thinking and acting which has nothing to do with the horizontal line and the directed time of history." However this may be in fact, it seems clear that Dante has staged, in symbol, the crossing of these two lines.

his triple rhyme Dante built everywhere into the structure of his creation a sign which the created universe itself everywhere displayed: the marks, the vestiges, left by a triune Architect. The poem, in fine, declares everywhere, with its terza rima, that it is an analogue to God's "poem," to God's book of the created universe. And even as all things in that universe reveal among themselves an order, so the parts of Dante's poem in its symmetries. Before now, too, we have recognized that the poet's style and his allegory both find their unique model in God's other book, in Holy Scripture. So that the poem is, in yet other significant respects, an analogue of God's way of building, and of God's way of writing. Before now, in short, we have known that this poet's work displayed analogy to God's work. And now shall we not see, in the pattern here discerned at the very center of the whole, the most striking manifestation yet of Dante's "imitation," and of the implicit canon of art by which a Christian poet did his work? For at the center of time and history, as God built time and history in His "poem," Christ comes and dies—and then will come again. So at the center of this Christian poet's work, we catch twice the reflection of the great model by which he built: at the center of the *Vita Nuova*, Beatrice's death like Christ's and her departure like an ascension; and at the center of the *Divine Comedy* Beatrice coming in what is her second coming as Christ will come in His. A human poem is thus by analogy participating in a divine poem, can be seen to be made in its image. In so doing, a poem does what all created things do in a Christian universe, a poem participates in true existence, in Being.[10] We shall be better readers of this poet's work when we shall have learned to follow out the unfolding of its form as the fulfillment of a necessary pattern; a pattern by which a Christian poem has its meaning—which, for this poem, at least, is that intelligibility by which it ultimately has its being.

[10] On the doctrine of analogy and of participation in being, consult E. Gilson, *The Spirit of Medieval Philosophy*, trans. Downes (New York, 1936), chapter on "Analogy, Causality and Finality" and *passim*.

Etienne Gilson

The Transfiguration of Beatrice

THE first point that we must remember, as we approach the problem, is that with Dante imagination had no part to play in the matter. As a Christian, he believed that the soul of Beatrice, like that of each and every human being, was an immortal substance whose final abode after the death of the body could only be heaven or hell. As a man, he knew from personal and unquestionable revelation that Beatrice was in heaven. These are the fundamentals of his problem as Dante himself conceived them; to understand how he solved it in this way we must attribute to them the same reality as he himself attributed to them. Some of his interpreters willingly accept the blest woman, but they refuse to remember that, to make a blest woman, the first essential is a woman; others do indeed believe in the real existence of this woman, but, less Christian than Dante, cannot take seriously the love of a poet for a blest woman. To these doubts no answer can be given, except that they render the *Divine Comedy* incomprehensible and dry up the source of the very beauty which makes us read it. If the sacred poem still lives, it is because its creator has peopled it only with living beings. Himself in the first place, by a unique decision which no poet had ever dared to take or has ever taken since. Then all the others, for not only have all the characters that move in it lived in history or legend, but they live in the poem more intensely than ever, in their individual essence as finally manifested by the inflexible law of divine justice. There is not a single dead man in the whole of the *Divine Comedy*.

That is why the text of Dante has nothing in common with any *Pélerinage de Vie Humaine, Roman de la Rose,* or other allegorical rubbish with its poverty of human stuff. When people tell us that "the *Roman de la Rose* ought to be studied here as Dante Alighieri is studied in the institutes of Rome and Tuscany," they are simply and solely confusing art with philology. When Jean de Meun chances to tell us of Charlemagne, Abelard and Heloise, we fall greedily upon these drops of water in his desert of allegories, but Slander, Giving-Too-Much and Mad Bounty soon reassert their rights, and Jean's few profoundly human lines on Guillaume de Loris and on himself are quickly buried beneath the chatter of Fear, Shame, Danger and Hypocrisy. The adventures of these proper names leave us cold and we no longer read what they say because it is completely and utterly insipid, but we shall always read Dante because the *Divine Comedy* is the story of a living being in the midst of other living beings and, among these living beings, there is none more real than Beatrice.

Let us note carefully that she is incomparably more so in the *Divine Comedy* than in the *Vita Nuova*. All social conventions being done away with, every equivocality of the flesh being removed, Dante and Beatrice no longer have to avoid each other in a square in Florence or content themselves with greetings exchanged from opposite sides of the street. As soon as they meet in Purgatory, they at last speak for the first time, and they do so in order to confess to each other all that has been

From E. Gilson, *Dante the Philosopher*, translated by David Moore, copyright 1949 by Sheed & Ward, Inc., New York; reprinted by permission of the publisher.

weighing on their hearts for so long. Beatrice knows that Dante has loved her for her womanly beauty: she tells him so at last. What reason could there now be for not speaking of these things? Dante had debased himself because of losing her, whereas the loss should have ennobled him: she tells him so, and he listens with downcast eyes, for his blush of shame is truly due to his being in this state *in her presence.* If it were only a question of personal remorse, Dante could have recourse to the art, so prevalent among men, of self-purification through forgetfulness, but so long as Beatrice knows and Dante knows that she knows, nothing can prevent his shame from persisting—nothing short of a request for pardon and the obtaining of it. That is why, in this "other life," which is still in a true sense "life," with no severance, no break, but, on the contrary, with a perfect continuity of essence under diversified conditions, the Beatrice whom Dante meets in Purgatory is not a duplicate of Beatrice any more than he himself is a duplicate of Dante; it is truly they themselves who meet again there and it is truly their own story that is continued. A number of Dante's interpreters are astonished or even shocked that he could say what he did of Beatrice the blessed if it is true that to him she was first a woman. Assuredly Dante exalted his Muse to the pinnacle of human grandeur, but did he go too far?

In order to approach the discussion of this problem through its most superficial aspect, we may fittingly note first that of all styles of language none was more familiar to Dante than that of the Scriptures. To him, as, for that matter, to his contemporaries, the Bible was not a book reserved exclusively for the use of priests when they conduct services in their churches. If the Biblical formulas have for him a special meaning, they owe it to the sacred origin of the book in which they are found; but every truly great event in human life, be it happy or tragic, has a sacred meaning of its own; to mark its true greatness we may

therefore express it in a sacred style of language. This is what Dante often did and, with the lack of false modesty for which he is well known, he applied the process to himself first.

If, we are told, Beatrice was really only a woman, Dante could not, "without blasphemy," have written of her as he did. To which the answer should be that we must resign ourselves to the facts: if they are such, Dante was a blasphemer. For it can hardly be doubted that he at all events was a real man; now it was he himself, and he himself as a pilgrim from the earthly city, *not* the blessed being that he might one day become, whom Dante fearlessly caused Virgil to greet in these terms: "Proud soul, blessed is she who conceived thee!" (Inf. VII, 44–45). In this *Beata colei che in te s'incinse!* who could fail to recognize the passage from the Gospel: *Beatus venter qui te portavit* (Blessed is the womb that bare thee) (St. Luke, XI, 27)? Here, then, is Dante's mother, whom he hardly knew and never mentioned, likened to the Virgin Mary, and Dante himself doing as much honor to his mother as if he had been Jesus Christ! Undoubtedly, it will be conceded that the poet never had this truly blasphemous intention. At the distance at which we are in time from his work, we cannot form an exact opinion of the impression produced on a contemporary of Dante by formulas of this kind. Were they in general use and did people speak the language of the Bible as those who are brought up on the sacred text are fond of doing? Was the expression a little too strong for the fastidious? Or was it frankly an error of taste? It is hard to tell. But these words have never been cast in Dante's teeth as a blasphemy. However high an opinion he may have had of himself, he never took himself for God.

The words that he uses in connection with Beatrice, or even in connection with other characters of less importance, should not be otherwise interpreted. Moreover, Dante did, on one occasion, reveal his se-

cret to us. In order to stimulate the belief
that he felt great sorrow at the departure
of a lady whom he had pretended to love,
Dante had decided to speak of her *alquanto
dolorosamente;* otherwise, he said, no one
would believe in his sham. What better way
to succeed than to write a *lamentanza,* in
other words a lamentation? So we see him
in the process of composing a lamentation
of Jeremiah; and what words has he not
chosen! The most sacred, because they directly apply to the passion of Christ:

> O ye that pass along the road of love,
> Pause and see
> If there be any grief as heavy as mine . . .
>   (*Vita Nuova,* VII)

This "road of love" introduced into the
text of Lamentations, I, 12, solely in order to deceive the reader, suggests that
Dante was not precisely scrupulous in these
matters. We shall not be surprised, after
this, that the poet has again assumed the
voice of Lamentations (I, 1) to announce
the death of Beatrice,[1] but we shall be still
less surprised that he has spoken to us of
Beatrice the blessed as in fact he has done.

The surest way to settle this problem
would perhaps be to begin by agreeing as
to what and what may not be said of a
soul that is blessed. To this question I offer
the following answer: We may praise it in
terms as lofty as we please, provided only
that we do not identify it with God. I was
almost about to add, "and even . . . !"—
for one could easily quote passages which,
if such an idea was not in their authors'
minds, seem nevertheless to express it. But
we need not go so far in order to understand Dante's words concerning Beatrice;
they can usually be explained simply by
reference to the power of grace, whose nature and effects no Christian can fail to
know.

Yet, to give ourselves the right to adopt
this principle of explanation, we must not
begin by laying down *a priori* what Dante
must have thought of Beatrice. If we were

to decide, for example, that Beatrice was
Revelation, there would be some reason for
saying that "in Dante's mind it would be a
profanation to make a real woman the symbol of Christian Revelation," [2] but there
would only be reason for saying so if to
Dante Beatrice really had been the symbol
of Revelation. The fact that she could not
be a woman if she symbolized that which
perhaps she does not symbolize does not
imply that she is not a woman. This is not
all. To draw a conclusion of any kind from
what are called "all the concrete notions
which form the outline of Beatrice *qua*
woman," we must begin by enumerating
them *all.*[3] That is not what is done, and it is
a pity. If one has failed to do it, one can
reach no conclusion from arguments like
the following, which has a hollow sound in
spite of its massive appearance: "The qual-
ifying terms bestowed by Dante on Beatrice are neither equivalent nor interchangeable. What Dante says, or appears to say,
of Beatrice *qua* lady may always be applied to Beatrice *qua* doctrine, but not *vice
versa.*" [4] In fact, this assertion is false, and,
if we confine ourselves to the first part of
it, it is even palpably so. If what Dante says
of Beatrice *qua* woman always applies to
theology, it must be said that theology was
born in Dante's lifetime, that it had well-
shaped limbs, that the father of theology
is dead, that theology itself followed this
excellent father to the grave, that its death
was bewailed by the whole town, that its
body has been interred, but that its soul is
in the heaven of the blessed. The truth is
that, to resort to the familiar language of
the author of this thesis, Beatrice *qua*
woman must indeed have an "outline," because she does not exist. If Revelation had
one in the *Divine Comedy,* it would only be
that of Beatrice *qua* woman, whose body,
grace and smile Revelation borrows;
whence we arrive, moreover, at the real
problem: Is it true that, *vice versa,* what

---

[1] Dante, *Vita Nuova,* XXVIII.

[2] P. Mandonnet, *Dante le Théologien,* p. 60.
[3] P. Mandonnet, op. cit., p. 63.
[4] P. Mandonnet, op. cit. p. 63–64.

Dante says of Beatrice *qua* doctrine may not always apply to Beatrice *qua* woman?

If this is true, it rests with those who maintain it to prove it. I would gladly help them to do so, but I do not remember a single passage in Dante concerning Beatrice which has seemed to me to raise such a theological problem. That is probably because I am simple enough to believe that a woman who enjoys the sight of God face to face is decidedly an excellent person. Not only that, but I believe also that a young Florentine girl who has received the grace of baptism is already, even before she has reached a state of beatitude, a being of supernatural dignity whose spiritual beauty passes imagination. The fact that I believe this is important only to myself; but Dante also believed it, and that is extremely important to the interpreter of his work. That is why I cannot admit that one "plumbs the depths of absurdity," if one thinks that Dante wrote of a Christian woman that she was "a miracle of the Trinity, surpassing all that nature and art can produce." This thesis is altogether strange, especially coming from a theologian and a theologian in whose mind Dante's thought and that of St. Thomas are confused. It is true that Dante is afterwards made to say: "So that between the first day and the last night of the world, God made nothing like her," a thing which, indeed, "cannot be said of any woman, since it implies superiority even to the angels." [5] But here our theologian's conclusion is a little too hasty, for there is at least one woman whom God created superior to the angels: the Virgin Mary.[6] And of Beatrice Dante never wrote this. In fact, he first of all said in the *Vita Nuova*, XXIX, that this Lady Beatrice was, *per similitudine*, a number 9, that is to say a miracle, whose root, that is to say the root of the miracle (cioè del miracolo), exists only in the Holy Trinity. Now St. Thomas teaches, like every theologian,

that man is an image of God. He does not even make any difficulty about admitting that in certain respects "the image of God exists more in man than in the angels." [7] If, as St. Thomas afterwards proves, that is true of every man, but especially of him who is *imago per conformitatem gratiae*,[8] and if this image of God exists in man "not only with respect to the divine nature but also with respect to the Trinity of the Persons," [9] it is not only Beatrice, but each one of us who, compared with the forces of nature and of art, *excedit omnem aliam naturam*.[10] So what, finally, is the root of all these marvels which transcend nature, if it is not the Trinity that creates and deifies?

Dante was therefore entirely right to glorify Beatrice—and moreover, in another passage—by praising her as one of the marvels of the Creator: *Questa è una maraviglia; che benedetto sia lo Segnore, che si mirabilmente sae adoperare! (Vita Nuova,* XXVI.) It is not of this passage, however, that Father Mandonnet is here thinking, but rather of the one which he elsewhere applies to Beatrice: "Between the last night and the first day (of the world) no work so great and magnificent ever . . . existed or will exist." [11] A decisive passage indeed, if it did apply to Beatrice; unfortunately, these words are uttered by Beatrice herself, and she is speaking of the mystery of the Incarnation and the Redemption. Thus, through allowing himself to be dominated by the fetish of system, Father Mandonnet has gone so far as to invent false passages

[5] P. Mandonnet, op. cit. p. 64.
[6] St. Thomas Aquinas, *Sum. Theol.*, Par. III, qu. 27, art. 5, Resp.
[7] St. Thomas Aquinas, op. cit. I, 99, 3, Resp.
[8] St. Thomas Aquinas, op. cit. I, 99, 4, Resp.
[9] St. Thomas Aquinas, op. cit. I, 99, 5, Resp.
[10] St. Thomas Aquinas, op. cit. Ia, IIae, 112, 1, Resp.
[11] Par., VII, 112–114; quoted by P. Mandonnet, *Dante le Théologien*, p. 213. On the same page, Father Mandonnet describes as inapplicable to a blest woman the following remark: "God alone can appreciate her thoroughly because He alone has a thorough knowledge of her." What else, then, could Dante have said, short of asserting that any creature may know another creature as thoroughly as its Creator knows it?

and even to cease to understand the obvious meaning of the true ones. He has lost in the process not only his Italian, but also his theology.

Above all, he has lost, what those who enter upon similar paths will lose with him, the deepest joy—one that is truly beatific of its kind—that communion with a genius through the medium of his work offers to the simplest reader. If one were deluding oneself in persisting in the assertion that a woman who is blessed is still a woman, and that she may remain so for the man who loves her, one would be guilty of a misinterpretation of Dante's work more inspired than that work itself. Such a thing has been known; but one cannot take the credit for adding to Dante what he himself never ceases to suggest. One is astonished to see a real woman undergo such a transfiguration; but unless she were real, how could Beatrice be transfigured? One is astonished again that a woman transfigured by glory should think, speak and love as a woman and that it should be as a woman that she is still loved; but if she were no longer a woman, how could she be a transfigured woman? What Dante here asks us to understand and to admit is precisely that, on the strength of the love that he bore her, Beatrice is exclusively marked out to be his intercessor with God. If God can win him back, it will be through her, and it is surely because Dante loves her still that God sends her to him. This man Dante will undoubtedly follow her, though he would follow no one else! And, in fact, he does follow her, in the character that she has now assumed—that of the mediator between his soul and God.

Such, indeed, combined with her glorification in heaven, is the transfiguration that Beatrice has undergone in the poet's soul. He himself says so time and time again, and it is because they have not taken him at his word that people have finally lost the meaning of his work. What kind of a person, then (they ask) is this Beatrice who, after coldly abandoning the young

Alighieri to wed Simone dei Bardi, makes herself ridiculous by addressing "scathing reproaches to Dante, who is lawfully married and the respectable father of a family!" And the most unconscionable thing is that after obtaining from Beatrice, from start to finish, two greetings in nine years, Dante "should still be infatuated with Beatrice, and more so than ever. What psychology!"[12] Alas! Yes, what psychology! But whose? And what kind of psychology can it be which does not appreciate that Beatrice the blessed is still a living woman— *quella viva Beatrice beata*[13]—but one transfigured into glory, and, when she meets Dante in purgatory, busied in her mind with something else besides involving him in a domestic scene at the cost of good sense and morality? She reproaches him with something quite different; through a failure to appreciate the fact, a misunderstanding has been inevitable as to the meaning of the entire work.

In order to understand Dante's attitude towards Beatrice, as, for that matter, that of Beatrice towards Dante, one need only remember that not all saints are in the calendar. Like so many other Christians, Dante thinks that, if he has a personal chance of salvation, it consists not in the intercession of great saints, men and women, of the whole Church, but in that of his own saint. Now let us not forget that Dante *knows* that Beatrice will live henceforth as a saint among saints. Why, then, should she not be to him what to so many Christians those beloved beings are, to whom they *know* that they can pray and to whom they do pray? As a means to the discovery of Love, how should they not first think of those whom they love still and by whom they are loved? In this man's past, the

[12] P. Mandonnet, *Dante le Théologien*, pp. 92–93. The argument had already been employed by E. V. Zappia, *Studi sulla "Vita Nuova" di Dante*, Rome, E. Loescher, 1904, p. 344. Zappia's book is discussed by M. Farbi, *La questione di Beatrice*, in *Problemi di critica dantesca*, Prima serie (1893–1918), Florence, Sansoni, 1934–XII, pp. 113–139.
[13] Dante, Convivio, II, 8.

mother whom he lost when so young—at about the age of six—is too indistinct a figure for him to think of turning to her. For him there is really no woman elect of God to whose personal intercession his love entitles him but this *Beatrice beata* whom, with that instinct which makes so many Christians pray to their mothers, Dante has made his mediator. If he undertakes a journey to the lands beyond the grave, what blessed soul does Dante hope to meet first to receive him on the threshold of heaven and lead him in? None but Beatrice. And she is, in fact, there. But Dante is not unaware of what he would first have to confess and expiate at this meeting. To find out, he had only to ask himself how, each time he felt that he was beneath her gaze, the associate of Forese Donati faced the soul of Beatrice:

> As those little ones, who, filled with shame and speechless,
> remain with their eyes fixed on the ground, listening,
> conscious of their guilt and contrite.
> so was I; and she said: "Since
> it is painful to thee to hear me, raise thy eyes:
> thy distress will only be the greater as thou beholdest me."
>
> (Purg., XXXI, 64–69)

But Dante well knows in whom he trusts, for when in the eighth heaven the sudden clamor of the triumphant spirits makes him sick with terror, like a frightened child that instinctively runs straight to her on whom it relies more than on anything in the world, Dante turns at once to Beatrice. But here nothing can take the place of his text:

> Oppresso di stupore, alla mia guida
> mi volsi, come parvol che ricorre
> sempre colà dove più si confida;
>
> e quella come madre che soccorre
> subito al figlio palido e anelo
> con la sua voce che il suol bien disporre
>
> mi disse: "Non sai tu che tu se' in cielo?"
>
> (Par., XXII, 1–7)

And what does she say to the pale, breathless little one—this succoring mother "whose voice is ever a solace to him"? Simply these divinely maternal words: "Thou knowest not, then, that thou art in heaven?" We are, I fear, rather far from the learned deductions from which it transpires that Beatrice never existed, save as a symbol of baptism, the clerical vocation, Minor Orders, continence, or the light of glory. But we are very close to Dante.

If Beatrice was not a real woman, loved by the poet so long as she dwelt on earth, still living in his heart after she had quitted this world, lost for a time during which his moral outlook was in the grip of a crisis which even threatened his genius, then rediscovered as a heavenly protectress whose intercession saved at once the man and the work bequeathed to us by the poet —if, I say, Beatrice was not this to Dante, it may be said that the *Divine Comedy* has systematically deceived us, and that it has unworthily deceived us by using the magic of the most splendid genius in order to make us believe in imaginary confessions, in which false lovers converse with feigned remorse and pretended griefs with a hope that has no object. Once again, this is not impossible, but to be credible, it would have to be proved. The fact that every attempt to prove it leads to flagrant contradictions of the words as they stand, then to distortion of the passages to which it is desired to give the form that they ought to have, finally to innumerable misinterpretations and justificatory sophisms, which abound as if of their own accord as soon as one enters upon this road, is perhaps enough to turn us from it.

There are two works in which Dante has not made a public confession: the *Vita Nuova* and the *Banquet*. If we only had these, we should have to take him for a chivalrous poet whom grief at the loss of his lady has led to philosophy. But we have others: the pieces of evidence constituted by the sonnets to Forese, and the public accusation of Dante by Beatrice in the *Divine*

Comedy. All these works were certainly written by the same man, but not at the same period of his life. Whatever estimate one forms of the sonnets, they fit in more easily with the fault of which the author of the *Divine Comedy* accuses himself than with the feeling that leads him to accuse himself of it. Such a personal work, in which the author is the chief actor, and in which we find him in the midst of a reality that may be verified in all its aspects, surrounded by friends and enemies whom he names and whom, moreover, we know, full of political passions and desires for vengeance, but also of forgiveness, remorse and hopes the objects of which we may identify—if that is not the whole truth regarding Dante (he himself did not know the whole of it and no man ever tells all that he knows of the truth about himself),

it is, at least, in the primary intention of its author, something of the truth about things which he himself regards as realities. If such is the case, the *Vita Nuova* certainly does not tell us of the downfall of a cleric or a theologian, but of the life of a young poet and his love for his Muse, whom he celebrates, loses and finds again transfigured. So there is here no question of theology. Even if, as I think—though it is debatable—the *Donna gentile* already symbolizes philosophy in this work, the matter in no way enlightens us as to the function which Dante attributes to it, apart from that of consoling him. To find out what Dante really thought of the philosophers and their wisdom, we must address ourselves to the work in which he himself says explicitly what he thinks of them—the *Banquet.*

Jefferson B. Fletcher

The "Three Blessed Ladies" of the *Divine Comedy*

WHEN Virgil first offers escape from the Dark Wood by the roundabout way through Hell and Purgatory, Dante accepts at once with grateful relief. But as the night shadows gather, his resolution falters. What Virgil proposed had indeed been done by mortal men. Virgil's own hero, Aeneas, had descended into Hell; St. Paul had been caught up into the Third Heaven; and both had come back to earthly life. But, exclaimed Dante,

"Io non Enea, io non Paolo sono." [1]

Virgil meets this pusillanimous doubt [2] by assuring Dante that divine aid will be given. Indeed, as Virgil will tell the various warders of the lower world—Charon, Minos, Plutus, Chiron, Malacoda—and, more respectfully, Cato, guardian of the Mount, the journey is willed on high. [3] He himself is but the messenger and instrument of Beatrice. She in turn had been incited to aid Dante by Lucia; Lucia by the Virgin Mary. [4] Mary alone seems to have seen Dante's plight, and to have acted on her own initiative. In the divine court, it was held, there are two jurisdictions,—one of justice, and one of mercy. Mary presides over the latter, and when she chooses to intervene, her decision is final. [5] Indeed, it is only filial obedience for Christ to yield to his mother's will, especially in a case of mercy. [6] To save her servants, she may not merely supplicate, but even maternally command her Son. [7]

The natural consequence of this extension of Mary's saving power was to make her the final arbiter of human fate. To gain her grace assured salvation; to lose it damnation. So St. Bernard advises Dante:

"Riguarda omai nella faccia ch'a Cristo
  più si somiglia, chè la sua chiarezza
  sola ti può disporre a veder Cristo." [8]

Fittingly, therefore, Dante's story of salvation starts with Mary's intervention in his mortal need, and ends with her securing for him in foretaste the final reward of beatitude. When Virgil rebukes Charon's natural reluctance to ferry the living Dante, by declaring it willed on high, he means that Mary wills it. So Cato later recognizes:

". . . se donna del ciel ti move e regge,
  come tu di', non c'è mestier lusinghe:
  bastiti ben che per lei ci richegge." [9]

Virgil had meant Beatrice, but she was sent by Mary. Moreover, St. Bernard applies to Mary the selfsame formula that Virgil had used with Charon and Minos. Virgil had said:

"Vuolsi così colà dove si puote
  ciò che si vuole." [10]

---

[1] *Inf*. II, 32.
[2] Ib. 43–48.
[3] *Inf*. III, 95–96; V, 23–24; VII, 10–12; XII, 88–89; XXI, 79–83; *Purg*. I, 52–84.
[4] *Inf*. II, 94–114.
[5] See Albertus Magnus, *De laudibus b. Mariae Virginis*, VI, xiii, 3. [The editor regrets that space limitations forbid reproducing the full quotations supplied by the author in his notes.]

[6] See St. Bonaventure, *Stimulus Amoris*, III, xix.
[7] Albert. Mag., op. cit. II, i, 21.
[8] *Par*. XXXII, 85–87. Cf. *Par*. XXXIII, 13–15.
[9] *Purg*. I, 91–93.
[10] *Inf*. III, 95–96; V, 23–24.

From *Symbolism of the Divine Comedy*, New York, Columbia University Press, 1921; reprinted, with substantial omissions, by permission of the publisher.

St. Bernard says:

> "Ancor ti prego, Regina che puoi
>   ciò che tu vuoli, . . ." [11]

Such verbal correspondences are in Dante's writings rarely accidental.

It is no mere poetic fancy, then, but soberly accepted faith for Dante to set the Virgin-Mother—so far as his, as everyman's, salvation is concerned—in the very place of the First Person of the Trinity, the Father

> "lo primo ed ineffabile Valore." [12]

In Dante's presentation she is, like God the Father, immobile. Unlike the miracle-working visitant of popular legend, she performs her acts of mercy vicariously. Regally, as befitting the Queen of Heaven and Empress of the Celestial, Terrestrial, and Infernal Kingdoms, she summons Lucia to her presence, and briefly commends the distressed Dante to her care:

> "Questa chiese Lucia in suo dimando
>   e disse: 'Or ha bisogno il tuo fedele
>   di te, ed io a te lo raccomando.'" [13]

Then, apparently, Mary does nothing more about it. Execution of her merciful providence is left to her agents, Lucia and Beatrice. She herself remains hieratically aloof in her heaven, watchful perhaps, but personally, it would seem, inactive. . . .

Dante merely voices contemporary belief, as defined by leading theological writers, when he attributes to the enthroned Mother of God effective control of human destiny. Whatever comes to us must have passed through her hands. She is accredited with an "omnipotence" coequal with Christ's; "for she is queen of that kingdom of which her Son is king, and king and queen enjoy the same prerogatives under the law." "Yet most excellently potent is she in the Church Triumphant,"—in the jurisdiction, that is, of man's salvation. In that jurisdiction, she is made to declare: "Mine is the power . . . to act as I see fit (*ad beneplacitum meum*), and to admit whom I will." [14]

The Mary of the *Divine Comedy* is often described as the "symbol of God's mercy." She is not that, but very God over man. Nor is her divine rôle merely one of mercy. She can be an "iron rod" to chastise the obdurate.[15] Effectively, therefore, the Virgin's favor is the one and supreme object of man's solicitude and solicitation. Homage may be dutifully paid to Father, Son, and Holy Spirit. Indeed, not to pay it would offend Mary herself. But the Trinity . . . becomes for the harassed Christian, practically an absentee inspiration. So Bonaventure changes to Mary's address the supplicatory psalm:

> "In te, Domina, speravi, non confundar in aeternum: in gratia tua suscipe me.
>
> Tu es fortitudo mea et refugium meum: consolatio mea et protectio mea.
>
> Ad te, Domina, clamavi, dum tribularetur cor meum: et exaudisti me de vertice collium aeternorum.
>
> Educas me de laqueo, quem absconderunt mihi: quoniam tu es adjutrix mea.
>
> In manus tuas, Domina, commendo spiritum meum: totam vitam meam et diem ultimum meum. Gloria Patri, etc." [16]

In the precise spirit of this converted psalm Dante represents his own rescue. "From the top of the eternal hills," Mary had heard and seen him lamenting in the "snare" of the dark monster-haunted wood. His rescuer is no mere allegorical symbol of an act of God, but a real person,—a living, acting, all-seeing, all-wise, and all-powerful divinity. Such was the faith of the age.

As soon as Dante, however, comes to dramatize Mary's ways and means of in-

---

[11] *Par.* XXXIII, 34–35.   [12] *Par.* X, 3.
[13] *Inf.* II, 97–99.

[14] Albert. Mag., op. cit. IV, xxx (*De omnipotentia Mariae*), 1.
[15] "Virgo Maria est virga ferrea daemonibus et incorrigibilibus." St. Bonaventure, *Spec. b. Mar. Virg.*, lect. XII.
[16] *Psalt. majus b. Mar. Virg.*, Ps. 30.

tervention, allegory would seem to begin. The curious way by which her aid is transmitted—almost as if through "military channels"—by Lucia to Beatrice, by Beatrice to Virgil, by Virgil to Dante himself, is of course dramatic fiction and allegory. But the precise signification is puzzling. Various interpretations have been offered by commentators, but the most currently accepted view is that summarized as follows by Professor Grandgent: "God in his mercy sends forth his illuminating grace to prepare the way for complete revelation, which will ensue as soon as the re-awakened voice of reason shall have made the sinner ready to receive it." [17]

This is an admirably clear and simple statement of the case. It represents truthfully, as I believe, the standard interpretation of the opening action of the poem. Of the "three ladies," the Virgin, "as generally in Christian thought, symbolizes divine Mercy"; Lucia is "the emblem of Grace—probably, as her name suggests, Illuminating Grace"; Beatrice "stands for Revelation, for which Dante's distorted mind must be prepared by Reason,"—that is, Virgil.

Now is this what Dante means? I ask the question in some embarrassment; for I realize that against the consensus of scholarly opinion a lone dissenter is certainly presumptuous and probably wrong. Still, the long chance is the interesting one. And besides, honestly I do not think this is what Dante means.

In the first place, the theological implication of the quoted interpretation is that God executes his own providence. The three ladies merely symbolize the three aspects of his executive act. But this is false to Dante's theology. In that, God knows and wills his providential plan, but deputes the execution of it to second causes, "intellectual creatures," in a descending scale.[18]

[17] *La Divina Commedia*, ed. and annot. by C. H. Grandgent, Heath & Co., 1913, p. 19.
[18] Cf. St. Thomas, *S. T.* I, xxii, 13. Cf. Ib. ciii, 6; *Contra Gent.* III, lxxvi-lxxix.

The Virgin, St. Lucia, Beatrice, Virgil, constitute such a descending scale of "intellectual creatures," who Dante says did personally influence him for good in the degree and kind of their respective illuminations. With regard to the Virgin there can be no question. Day and night, he says, he invoked her name. So to do was the bounden duty and the ground of hope of every good Catholic. Dante's dependence on the actual St. Lucia is more doubtful. He may have invoked her to cure his poor eyesight. At least, such healing-power was accredited to her. He may have invoked her aid in more spiritual issues. But the suspicion arises that her personal prominence in the story of his redemption is due rather to the derivation of her name from *luce*, light, and the neat way this signification fitted in with her healing-power, especially if this power were conceived to extend to spiritual vision as well as to physical. For light is the natural aid to vision. If this suspicion be well grounded, undoubtedly the character of Lucia is from the outset preponderantly symbolic. In other words, the living saint's personality has been merged into its special virtue, and the virtue itself reduced to its theoretic principle. The actual light-giver to the dim of sight becomes the symbol of Light itself, physical and spiritual. If Beatrice, on the other hand, was to and for Dante what he says she was, then on earth and from heaven her influence upon him was concretely personal. *She* helped him, not something else she might "stand for." Even if Dante invented her, he invented her as a personality, and not as a personification. But in her immortal personality, as in any living spiritual organism, there would be a hierarchy of powers, with one supreme and controlling power, one that gave form and direction to all the rest. To say that by such a dominant power, or characteristic, she influenced Dante, is not to treat it in abstraction from the powers over which it was dominant. A rudder steers a ship, but a rudder cannot steer without a ship. Yet, although the actual Beatrice influenced Dante from heaven, her individual influence could not, like Mary's, be represented as universal. It would have been insanity of praise to set up his lady, however glorious among women, as a divinity regulating all mankind. She herself had promised:

"Sarai meco senza fine cive
di quella Roma onde Cristo è Romano." [19]

She too was but a private citizen in the kingdom of heaven. Therefore, to make his redemption through her serviceable as an example to his fellow-men, he must, so to speak, de-individualize her, reveal to them what power, incarnate in her, was itself universally salutary. In fine, Beatrice becomes a symbol, not for Dante's rescue, but for the rescue of mankind. There remains Virgil. An obvious distinction between his case and that of the three ladies is that they are in heaven, and Virgil in hell. The mere fact of being damned, however, would not make Virgil's actual spirit ineligible as an instrument of God for man's benefit.[20] And it would be hazardous to deny categorically that one of Dante's time and faith might not have entertained the idea of actual supernatural aid from his beloved master's spirit. Was not he, Dante, admitted sixth in that "fair school" of which Virgil was master? But I do not insist upon the point. At least, the spirit of Virgil lived and spoke to Dante in immortal poetry, in that "right speaking," upon which, as honoring him and all that heard him, Beatrice relied for Dante's moral correction.[21] Such an influence is neither allegory nor fiction. And there can be no doubt that Dante was deeply stirred by the noble character, the humane wisdom and sweet reasonableness of Virgil as revealed in his writings. These qualities appear in the character of the *Comedy*. Dante's Virgil is no mere symbol of Reason in the abstract; he is, in the richest sense, an "all-round man,"—one, that is, whose whole character is true-centered on reason. Indeed, as will be argued more fully hereafter, Virgil's efficacy is more than that of natural reason. Otherwise he could not lead Dante to Beatrice, could not, in fact, get out of Limbo.

Thus, as it seems to me, the standard interpretation I have quoted, errs in attributing to God a direct action which according to Catholic theology he does not exercise, in ignoring the all-dominant divinity of the Virgin, and in empoverishing the rôles especially of Beatrice and Virgil. Even Lucia, I think, has a richer and more complex signification than merely and statically that of "Illuminating Grace."

But another kind of objection seems to lie against the standard interpretation. It does not work out right. We are justified in expecting from a writer so meticulously scrupulous as Dante an exact correspondence between the literal narrative and the symbolic implication. But if "God in his mercy sends forth his illuminating grace to prepare the way for complete revelation," surely the proper recipient of grace is the sinner, Dante. In point of fact, Lucia, or Illuminating Grace, does not at this time go out to Dante at all, but to Beatrice. And if "Beatrice stands for Revelation," in what sense can Revelation receive illuminating grace? Would it not be "carrying coals to Newcastle"? Then Beatrice descends to Virgil in hell. But if Virgil receives revelation, how can Virgil stand for Reason-without-revelation? Once more, if Beatrice signifies the "complete revelation which will ensue as soon as the reawakened voice of reason shall have made the sinner ready to receive it," how happens it that the final rapture of revelation comes to Dante when Beatrice is no longer with him?

Now I hope I have made it clear that I am impugning not the personal interpretation of a particular scholar, but the standard interpretation, the interpretation given in nearly all the current commentaries. And I have the temerity to believe it pos-

[19] *Purg.* XXXII, 101–102.
[20] Cf. St. Thomas, *S. T.* II–II, clxxii, 5–6.
[21] *Inf.* II, 112–114.

sible to put finger on the principal point where this standard interpretation goes astray. It is perfectly true that the Christian has two sources of knowledge, to wit, his own faculty of reason, and revelation through Christ. It is true also that in the sinner's mind reason is dethroned, or at least corrupted, and that by such a mind revelation would be misunderstood and perverted. . . . It follows then that the sinner's "distorted mind" must be "prepared—or rather repaired—for revelation" by the re-enthronement of reason. So Virgil, as Reason, aided by Lucia as Illuminating Grace, prepares Dante's mind to receive Beatrice. It seems to follow, therefore, that Beatrice must be Revelation.

And it might follow if Dante's reception of Beatrice, his spiritual possession of her, were the consummating end. But it is not. She even warns him against such an idea:

"Chè non pur ne' miei occhi è Paradiso." [22]

The true consummating end is God's own self-revelation to a mind prepared to receive the *"fulgore,"* the effulgence, of that overwhelming illumination.[23] Beatrice is for Dante a means to that end, an instrument of God's in the execution of that providential plan. No doubt she was the instrument of grace that touched him most nearly, but her very influence over him was due to the focussing in her of all the lights of heaven, which are also God's instruments. The resulting splendor of her beauty, physical and spiritual, awoke in him love of her. Then the recognition that this her splendor was the radiated reflection of still diviner beings, of the saints, and of the angels above the saints, and of the Virgin above the angels, and of the Godhead above the angels, enlarged at last his love of her to love of God.[24] And to this love of God, this charity, so made perfect in Dante himself, is due the rewarding revelation of God, beatitude—by him foretasted. For the one thing essential to beatitude is perfect charity.[25]

Beatrice's training, then, is a training in charity. But how? She herself implies the answer:

"Ne impetrare spirazion mi valse,
    con le quali ed in sogno ed altrimenti
    lo rivocai; sì poco a lui ne calse.
Tanto giù cadde che tutti argomenti
    alla salute sua eran già corti,
    fuor che mostrargli le perdute genti." [26]

Her earlier "revelations" had failed of their purpose; her later ones—of the "lost folk" —sufficed for his rescue. And then, after he had paid his "scot of penitence that sheddeth tears," [27] had passed through purgatory, and crossed Lethe, he received the progressive revelations of the blest folk which culminated in the revelation of God himself.

I might appear to be throwing away my case. If Beatrice's training was by successive "revelations," is not her symbolic function revelation? And is not the standard interpretation therefore right? Yet, let us consider a little more closely.

In the first place, she says that she "obtained" revelations, not *gave* them. The revelation itself did not come from any power of hers. Would it not, then, be a singular conception of symbolism which should make her represent a power which she had not? In the second place, I have been using the term "revelation,"—as I think the majority of commentators use it,—in a loose and untechnical way. But Dante never uses philosophical and theological terms in a loose and untechnical way. And "revelation" in the technical theological sense is carefully defined by his master, St. Thomas. "A revelation includes a vision, and not conversely; for whenever things are seen, the intelligence and signification of which are obscure to the seer, then it is a vision only, such as was the vision of Pharaoh and Nebuchadnezzar, . . . but when togeth-

---

[22] *Par.* XVIII, 21. Cf. *Par.* XXIII, 70–72.
[23] Cf. *Par.* XXXIII, 140–142.
[24] Cf. *Purg.* XXXI, 22–27.

[25] "Perfectio charitatis est essentialis beatitudini." St. Thomas, *S. T.* I–II, iv, 8, 3m.
[26] *Purg.* XXX, 133–138.
[27] Ib. 144–145.

er with the vision is had the signification and intelligence of those things which are seen, this is revelation." [28] There are, accordingly, two factors in any genuine revelation,—(1) the vision or inspiration given, and (2) understanding of it by the recipient. The earlier visions and inspirations obtained for Dante by Beatrice,—those narrated in the *New Life*,—were not obscure or defective in themselves. If they had been, her rebuke would have been unjust. The defect was in him, in his power of understanding. Indeed, later, under analogous circumstances, she tells him so.[29] So, if the later visions,—those recounted in the *Divine Comedy*,—proved, as they did, to be efficacious, to be genuine revelations, it must be because Dante himself had become enabled to interpret them. His faculty of understanding must have been improved. That improvement was her work. Of her own power she could not produce the vision, the first factor of revelation; but it was her power that actualized the second factor, his power to comprehend, and so to profit by, the vision. And this, in fact, he acknowledges to be the very sum and substance of his obligation to her. In his last solemn words to her, he says:

"Di tante cose quante io ho vedute,
    dal tuo potere e dalla tua bontate
    riconosco la grazia e la virtute." [30]

Or, more briefly, he owes the efficacy of his visions to her power.

The conclusion seems to me unescapable. The power or virtue which Beatrice exerts for Dante's good, and which—taken in itself as universally salutary—she symbolizes, is not Revelation, but one that, communicated, can by understanding transform visions, "things seen," *into* revelation. To miss this distinction, to confuse this power with Revelation, is like confusing the steam with the engine. What then is this power?

[28] II *Cor.* xii, 1.
[29] *Purg.* XXXIII, 64–75.
[30] *Par.* XXXI, 82–84.

There are two ways of answering this question,—one by the theological necessity of the case, the other from intimations and implications of Dante's own text. Naturally, both ways should lead to the same result; and it might be considered more natural and more final to enquire what he means from what he says than to force—perhaps—his words into conformity with any theological dogma. But Dante is an economist—in the theological sense—of truth. He writes "*ad utilitatem*," saying in effect to his reader what Love in the vision of the New Life had said to him: "*Non domandar più che utile ti sia.*" He omits to label his symbolic characters and meanings, because so to do would have been, not only useless, but even worse than useless. . . . Their symbolic significations follow from their respective functions in a highly complex system of ideas. Really to understand them, the reader must first understand this system. So, lest the incompetent reader may be misled into thinking he understands when he cannot, Dante deliberately veils his deeper meanings by insinuating them enigmatically. It is the avowed practice of medieval theologians when addressing intellectually mixed audiences. The experts can read the riddles; the others are mercifully and prudently spared mischievous misunderstandings. Safely to read Dante's enigmas, therefore, we must, as best we may, take the approach of the philosophical and theological expert.

Now theologically speaking, there are two resources given to man for interpreting the "intelligence and signification" of "things seen." One is by the "use of reason"; the other, "through a certain connaturalness with the things to be judged." Both are called wisdom; but the wisdom acquired by the use of reason proceeds discursively from the data of sense, and is therefore of itself incompetent to judge of divine things, which are beyond sense. The wisdom, on the other hand, which proceeds from connaturalness with divine things is a gift of the Holy Spirit. It is not acquired, but infused. And its procedure is not by discursive inference, but by a "divine," and therefore infallible, "instinct." Moreover, if this divine gift of wisdom has its essence in the intellect, or faculty of judgment, it has its cause in the will, to wit, in charity.[31]

The visions and inspirations obtained by Beatrice for Dante were of "divine things." His judgment of them had three stages: (1) by imperfect use of reason,—his rational faculty being impeded by passion; (2) by perfect use of reason,—symbolized by the guidance of Virgil aided by divine light, or gratuitous grace; (3) by the "divine instinct," or intuition, of the *gift* of wisdom, vouchsafed to all who have charity, and symbolized by the personal guidance of Beatrice. The symbolic distinction, then, between Virgil and Beatrice is not between Reason and Revelation, but between Reason humanly perfected in "acquired Wisdom" (*Sapientia adquisita*) and Reason divinely perfected in "infused Wisdom" (*Sapientia infusa*). The former reaches beyond the things of sense only by abstraction and discursive logic; the latter has intuitive cognizance of divine things by a "certain connaturalness" with them.

As St. Thomas states, the *essence* of this infused wisdom, of wisdom as a gift, is in the intellect; its *cause* is in the will,—that is, in charity. In other words, infused wisdom is of an intellect actualized by charity, —or, more briefly still, of an intellect of love. Such, then, is the deeper meaning of the famous opening address of the canzone:

"Donne ch'avete intelletto d'amore,"

"Ye ladies—or more generally, spirits— that have the intellect of love." [32] Also is explained how and why in the responsive canzone put into their mouths, they, like Dante, acknowledge that their infused wisdom is due to Beatrice's influence. She, as they say,

is *"la fontana d'insegnamento,"* [33] which *"di noi ciascuna fa saccente."* And in view of his faithful service, they promise Dante to intercede for him with Love, and to recommend him to Love.

The deeper insight of an intellect actualized by love is explicitly alluded to by Beatrice herself in reference to the mystery of God's sacrifice for man:

"Questo decreto, frate, sta sepulto
    agli occhi di ciascuno il cui ingegno
    nella fiamma d'amor non è adulto." [34]

And Dante's definition of the nature of his poetic inspiration is made in direct conjunction with the line of the canzone quoted by Bonagiunta:

"Ma di' s'io veggio qui colui che fuore
    trasse le nuove rime, cominciando:
    'Donne ch'avete intelletto d'amore,'
Ed io a lui: 'Io mi son un che, quando
    amor mi spira, noto, ed a quel modo
    che ditta dentro, vo significando.' " [35]

His poetry was due to his intellect having become an *"intelletto d'amore,"* operating by "divine instinct." It will be remembered that his tongue spoke the line, "Donne ch'avete intelletto d'amore," "quasi come per se stessa mossa."

The ladies of the responsive canzone promised to recommend the faithful Dante to "Love." They must mean Beatrice herself, since she alone could reward her servant. Also, in the *New Life*, Love himself, personified, announced the virtual identity of Beatrice and himself: *"Chi volesse sottilmente considerare, quella Beatrice chiamerebbe AMORE, per molta simiglianza che ha meco."* [36] Here, and constantly also in the *Divine Comedy*, Beatrice would represent, or symbolize Love,—that is the holy love which is charity. I have just seemingly demonstrated, on the other hand, that she

[31] Cf. St. Thomas, *S. T.* II–II, xlv, 2, c.
[32] The more usual translation, "intelligence of love," will serve if "intelligence" is understood in the active sense of the faculty of intelligence.

[33] Canz. *Ben-aggia-l'amoroso,* ll. 64–65. The author of this canzone, whether Dante or not, certainly understood Dante.
[34] *Par.* VII, 58–60.
[35] *Purg.* XXIV, 49–54.
[36] *V. N.* XXIV, 41–43.

symbolizes the Intellect of Love. The ambiguity is a matter of two facets of one crystal, two aspects of a concrete, and therefore multiple, symbol. . . .

The efficacy of Beatrice as Love was to kindle a like love in Dante. And at first this normal effect followed. But because he yielded to baser desires, connaturalness was lost between his love and the Love she represented. So, losing charity, he lost the "divine instinct" to interpret his saving inspirations, and went from bad to worse. Yet in the renouncement of his desired reward of her salutation, charity was rekindled, and a "new and nobler" chapter in his young life opened. For charity gives and asks not, and would rather love than be loved. The process repeats itself in his later falling away with the "compassionate lady" and subsequent repentance, until at last his thought rises to Beatrice in heaven, moved by a "new Intelligence" which Love infuses. This new intelligence caused by love,—or intellect of love,—is potentially capable of comprehending the divine things which Beatrice may tell or show him. As yet, however, it is weak, as his new-born charity is incipient only. To develop his new insight he must "study," that is, meditate upon divine things—things connatural with her. The beauty of these increases his charity, and increased charity strengthens his intellect. This reciprocal process is the spiritual dialectic of the *Paradise*.

In the *Divine Comedy*, the power of Beatrice is from the beginning recognized as love. Love, she tells Virgil, moved her to descend into hell for Dante's sake. In his reply, Virgil addresses her:

"O donna di virtù, sola per cui
l'umana spezie eccede ogni contento
di quel ciel che ha minor li cerchi sui." [37]

This address is tantamount to calling Beatrice Love; for love of God, or charity, is the virtue by which the human race is exalted to the Empyrean. And presently Lucia re-enforces the point by calling Beatrice

"*loda di Dio vera*." "True praise of God" is charity, love of God. Perfectly to rejoice in God, says St. Bonaventure, is to love him in our hearts, to praise him with our lips, and to bear witness to him in our works. But, as Christ said, the fulfilment of all rejoicing is to love God. The rejoicing of the loving heart is the root, of which the rejoicing of the lips and the rejoicing by works are the branches. Again, of all creatures, the Seraphim, interpreted as the "burning in love," [38] most intimately praise God. . . . Over and over Dante repeats it in ever new connections. God is Love; Beatrice is Love; therefore she, drawing him to herself, thereby draws him to God. She declares it:

"Per entro i miei disiri,
che ti menavano ad amar lo bene
di là dal qual non è a che si aspiri," etc.[39]

. . . Her first instrument, Virgil or Reason, in effect syllogizes her identity with sacred love. Free choice is given to man between his loves, sacred and profane.

"Quest' è il principio, là onde si piglia
ragion di meritar in voi, secondo
che buoni e rei amori accoglie e viglia." [40]

So choice and following of sacred love is the "ground of merit" by which man attains beatitude. After perilous dalliance with profane loves, seduced by "present things with their false pleasure," [41] Dante finally chose Beatrice, and is now following her securely towards beatitude. Therefore, she whom he has chosen and follows, is, or represents, sacred love. Virgil, limited to discursive reasoning, can only infer; Bernard, Beatrice's second and final instrument, Contemplation in the highest grade, recognizes and openly declares the identity:

"Accio chè tu assommi
perfettamente," disse, "il tuo cammino,
a che prego ed amor santo mandommi,

[37] *Inf.* II, 76–78.

[38] Cf. St. Thomas, *Cont. Gent.* III, lxxx.
[39] *Purg.* XXXI, 22–24.
[40] *Purg.* XVIII, 64–66. Cf. *Purg.* XVII, 103–105.
[41] *Purg.* XXXI, 34–35.

vola con gli occhi per questo giardino;
  che veder lui t'acconcerà lo sguardo
  più al montar per lo raggio divino." [42]

Beatrice, that is, *"amor santo,"* "sacred love," sent him. In the second tercet is again illustrated how, looking on the beauteous flowers in the garden of heaven, Dante will kindle to greater love, and greater love the more will sharpen his spiritual sight.

Again, I may outline, as briefly as may be, a longer and more complicated chain of evidence towards the symbolic identity of Beatrice and Charity. Following the sacred Love which is Beatrice, Dante even in this life reaches to a momentary foretaste of beatitude. Like St. Paul, he is "caught up to the third heaven," and there sees God "face to face." But although his human faculty is incapable of retaining, still less of communicating, this wholly supersensuous knowledge, yet he does know, after his spirit has redescended to earth, that his human will is wholly conformed to God's will, and has chosen forever the sacred Love which is of God, and of which Beatrice is reflection and likeness. [43] As Bonaventure said, this Love of God and from God which is Charity "gives and asks not." Possessing it, or rather possessed by it, Dante is drawn down from his contemplative rapture to active service. For to suspend contemplation to serve others belongs to the highest perfection of charity. [44] Like Paul, he becomes an apostle to men of the love with which he, like Beatrice, has become one. The *Divine Comedy*, lesson and example of how man is saved by love, is the message of his apostleship, and—because Beatrice is Love—its preachment of love is also praise of her. So preaching, he was fulfilling her dictate:

"Tu nota; e sì come da me son porte,
  così queste parole segna ai vivi
  del viver ch'è un correr alla morte." [45]

And he himself now knows that her dictate and the continuing dictation of Love in his own mind are one and the same:

"Io mi son un che, quando
  Amor mi spira, noto, ed a quel modo
  che ditta dentro, vo significando." [46]

Moreover, his following of Love's dictation is authorized by the first and right vicar of Christ. [47]

In the retrospect, also, enigmatic sayings are made clear. Virgil's warning at the beginning, that Dante may not ascend the "delectable mount" by the direct way holds true for him now that he is redeemed even as it did for him a sinner, though in a different spirit. For the virtuous man, the direct way is by the contemplative life. But so far as one is wholly absorbed in contemplation, he may neglect the temporal needs of others. So the Virtues, of whom Charity is the leader, turned his absorbed gaze from Beatrice to the left, exclaiming *"Troppo fiso!"* [48] Attention to the "left" is to the duty of the active life, especially of provision for others. [49] So Beatrice herself had foretold that he must remain a while longer a "forester" in the forest of this world. [50] Had she herself not descended into hell for his sake? She was indeed immune from the evils of hell, but then so Dante now was from the beasts, the vices, which infest this dark forest. To hunt them down "for the sake of the world that evil lives," he must abide in patient service—and even suffering. For, as he had been repeatedly warned in his upward journey, in spite of his redemption—or rather because of it—the forest of this life must become darker than ever for him. Only, it will no longer be the darkness of his own sinfulness, but the darkness of tribulation and sorrow, which shall overshadow him even as the apostle Paul. To this threat, as foretold by the old warrior, his ancestor, Cacciaguida, Dante

---

[42] *Par.* XXXI, 94–99.
[43] *Par.* XXXIII, 140–145.
[44] Cf. St. Thomas, *S. T.* II–II, clxxxii, 1, c.
[45] *Purg.* XXXIII, 52–54.

[46] *Purg.* XXIV, 52–54.
[47] *Par.* XXVII, 64–66.
[48] *Purg.* XXXII, 1–9.
[49] Cf. St. Thomas, *S. T.* I–II, cii, 4, 6^m.
[50] *Purg.* XXXII, 100–102.

had opposed a front of moral stoicism, declaring himself

"Ben tetragono ai colpi di ventura,—"[51]

a four-square tower whose walls are the cardinal virtues. But although stoic virtue may offer a brave front to persecution, none the less it feels the bitterness thereof. Beatrice offers, on the other hand, the true consolation of Christian love and trust in God, of charity. And her loving voice, and the love in her eyes, release Dante from every care, from every desire—

"Fin che il piacere eterno, che diretto
    raggiava in Beatrice, dal bel viso
    mi contentava col secondo aspetto."[52]

"The eternal bliss" directly reflected upon her face is, as Dante has just said, love, and love is in fact "the second aspect" of "eternal bliss," or beatitude:

"Si fonda
l'esser beato nell'atto che vede
non in quel ch'ama, che poscia seconda."[53]

Finally, Dante's last thanksgiving and prayer to Beatrice sums the fourfold effect of her charity upon him and within him.[54] (1) By her loving mercy reaching down to the hell of his perverse spirit, she has lifted him up to *hope*. (2) By her grace and goodness she has shown him what God, the Highest Good, is like, and so confirmed his *faith*. (3) By the heat of her charity, she has kindled in him *charity*, and charity maketh free. (4) Let her "magnificence" so watch over and keep his healed soul that it may be released from the body "pleasing" to her who is perfect charity. She hears and fulfils his desire; for through her own "prayer and holy love," transmitted by Bernard, the Virgin, dispenser of beatitude, grants Dante the vision of God, by which his "desire and will" are, like Beatrice's own, altogether moved by perfect charity. In other words, by direct revelation of God he is assured of being in a state of grace, and therefore pleasing to Beatrice. It may

be repeated, by the way, that although this final and supreme revelation is obtained for Dante by Beatrice, she for that very reason must symbolize not it, but the means to it; and again the means to the revelation of God, which is beatitude, is charity. That beatific revelation is vouchsafed to living man only "by special privilege" in the strongest sense of the term. The "Dante" of the *Comedy*, accordingly, by no means represents typical Man. On the contrary, thanks to the "miracle" Beatrice, his grace is miraculous. The spirits he meets marvel at it, and felicitate him on it. In view of the magnitude of her benefaction, therefore, Beatrice is fitly called magnificent.

. . . But Beatrice represents Charity in only one aspect of her symbolic function. Thus, having charity, she possesses also the gifts of the Holy Spirit, and accordingly her influence illumines the mind as well as kindles the will. In a secondary aspect, therefore, she represents "intellectual light" (*lumen intellectuale*), and is frequently hailed as such. So, for instance, Virgil to Dante:

"Veramente a così alto sospetto
    non ti ferma, se quella nol ti dice,
    che lume fia tra il vero e l'intelletto."[55]

This passage has been cited as confirmation of Beatrice as Revelation. But, as has been shown, there is no revelation, in the right sense of the term, unless the recipient is capable of understanding it. At the time when Virgil speaks, Dante's mind is not "lighted," but "smokes."[56] What Beatrice does is to infuse, through charity, the "intellectual light" which she herself, possessing, represents. In one more aspect, Dante becomes connatural with her.

Among other passages in which Beatrice figures specifically as the light-giver, there is one of capital importance, namely, that in which, after his immersion in Lethe, Dante is vouchsafed Beatrice's direct glance and her smile. The four cardinal, or moral, Virtues declare themselves:

---

[51] *Par.* XVII, 24.   [52] *Par.* XVIII, 16–18.
[53] *Par.* XXVIII, 109–111.   [54] *Par.* XXXI, 79–90.
[55] *Purg.* VI, 43–45.   [56] Cf. *Par.* XXI, 100.

"Noi sem qui ninfe, e nel ciel semo stelle.
  Pria che Beatrice discendesse al mondo,
  fummo ordinate a lei per sue ancelle." [57]

"By charity the acts of all the other virtues are ordered to the final end," beatitude.[58] Figuratively, therefore, the other virtues may be regarded as "handmaids" of Charity. They are then handmaids of Beatrice as Charity in two senses, according as we take the phrase *"discendesse al mondo"* to mean her mortal birth, or her descent from heaven to Dante in the earthly paradise. In the first case, since her dominant trait was predestined to be charity, her other virtues are ancillary to that. In the second case, in her, as a glorified spirit, while charity is only intensified, the moral virtues persist merely formally, or in principle. For *prudence* in heaven is without danger of error, *fortitude* is without evil to be endured, *temperance* without incitement of lust; and the one act of *justice* is submission to God. . . . But while the moral virtues so have no material function for the glorified Beatrice, their formal perfection affects Dante as model and inspiration. And thus they are handmaids of her charity towards him, leading him to her eyes, through which her charity radiates, kindling and illumining his soul. In other words, upon the charity so infused into him follow the gifts of intelligence (*intellectus*) and wisdom (*sapientia*), giving him an insight above reason into the mystery of the Incarnation, the principle of salvation. So charity deepened, faith fortified, and hope renewed, he is led by these three holy Virtues to realize Beatrice's "second beauty," her smile,—or beatitude reflected in her. For that end to which the three holy virtues lead is beatitude. . . . Since, according to the physiological-psychology of love,[59] her love—which is charity—proceeds on the ray from her eyes through his into his heart, there kindling charity, so her eyes may poetically be regarded as the efficient cause of the effect of

charity in him, or gift of wisdom, by which he more intimately knows God. Or, by ellipsis, he may fitly call her eyes *"principio di Amore,"* [60] and, in reference to her having the gift of wisdom, "demonstrations of wisdom, by which truth is seen with certainty." [61] . . . Again, the end, or final cause, of his infused grace of charity is union with God, or beatitude. That supremely desirable consummation is what draws, or persuades, his will, as the splendor of a light draws the moth. So, since again according to love-psychology, the beloved's smile signifies the "end of love," or reward of her favor,[62] by which the lover is persuaded to service, so, once more by elliptical statement, Beatrice's smile is called the "persuasions of Wisdom, by which is demonstrated the interior light of Wisdom under a certain veil." [63] To Dante, now in full conduct of the three holy virtues, however, Beatrice accords the grace of removing this veil. His intuitive power is proportioned to his increased charity, and his eyes are of one "whose wit is in the flame of love adult." [64] Therefore they are able to look upon Wisdom's end, Truth, directly, as the "splendor of the living light eternal," and no longer merely upon its "pallid" reflection in the "Parnassus well" of human reasoning. So the "new intelligence which Love has given," [65] wisdom as a divine gift and effect of charity, transcends his old wisdom, that was but an "intellectual virtue." Reciprocally, the new-seen splendor of Truth strengthens his love of it anew, and that new-strengthened love will induce new and deeper insight, and this cumulative process is renewed until, God's infinity directly seen and loved, there is no farther to go:

"Di là dal qual non è a che si aspiri." [66]

---

[57] *Purg.* XXXI, 106–108.
[58] St. Thomas, *S. T.* II–II, xxiii, 8, c.
[59] Cf. *Conv.* II, xi, 32–48.

[60] *V. N.* XIX, 133.
[61] *Conv.* III, xv, 12–15: Cf. *Inf.* X, 130–132: her eyes "see all."
[62] *V. N.* XIX, 133–134.
[63] *Conv.* III, xv, 16–18.
[64] *Par.* VII, 59–60.
[65] *V. N.* XLII, 49–50.
[66] *Purg.* XXXI, 24.

Allen Tate

The Symbolic Imagination:
A Meditation on Dante's Three Mirrors

IT IS RIGHT even if it is not quite proper to observe at the beginning of a discourse on Dante, that no writer has held in mind at one time the whole of the *Divine Comedy:* not even Dante, perhaps least of all Dante himself. If Dante and his Dantisti have not been equal to the view of the whole, a view shorter than theirs must be expected of the amateur who, as a writer of verses, vainly seeks absolution from the mortal sin of using poets for what he can get out of them. I expect to look at a single image in the *Paradiso,* and to glance at some of its configurations with other images. I mean the imagery of light, but I mean chiefly its reflections. It was scarcely necessary for Dante to have read, though he did read, the *De Anima,* to learn that sight is the king of the senses and that the human body, which like other organisms lives by *touch,* may be made actual in language only through the imitation of *sight.* And sight in language is imitated not by means of "description"—*ut pictura poesis*—but by doubling the image: our confidence in its spatial reality is won quite simply by casting the image upon a glass, or otherwise by the insinuation of space between.

I cannot undertake to examine here Dante's double imagery in all its detail, for Dante's light alone could lead us into complexities as rich as life itself. I had almost said richer than life, if by life we mean (as we must mean) what we ourselves are able daily to see, or even what certain writers have seen, with the exception of Shakespeare, and possibly of Sophocles and Henry James. A secondary purpose that I shall have in view will be to consider the dramatic implications of the light imagery as they emerge at the resolution of the poem, in Canto XXXIII of the *Paradiso.* These implications suggest, to my mind, a radical change in the interpretation of the *Divine Comedy,* and impel me to ask again: What kind of poem is it? In asking this question I shall not be concerned with what we ordinarily consider to be literary criticism; I shall be only incidentally judging, for my main purpose is to describe.

In *Purgatorio* XXX Beatrice appears to Dante first as a voice (what she says need not detain us here), then as light; but not yet the purest light. She is the light of a pair of eyes in which is reflected the image of the gryphon, a symbol of the hypostatic union, of which she herself is a "type." But before Dante perceives this image in her eyes, he says: "A thousand desires hotter than flame held my eyes bound to the shining eyes. . . ." [1] I see no reason to suppose that Dante does not mean what he says. *Mille disiri più che fiamma caldi* I take to be the desires, however interfused by this time with courtly and mystical associations,

[1] Quotations in English from the *Divine Comedy* are from the translation by Carlyle, Okey, and Wicksteed, in the Temple Classics edition. Here and there I have taken the liberty of neutralizing certain Victorian poeticisms, which were already archaic in that period.

From A. Tate, *Collected Essays,* Denver, The Swallow Press, 1959; copyright 1953, 1959 by Allen Tate. Reprinted (with omission of a longish passage) by permission of the publisher. This essay was first read at Boston College under the auspices of the Candlemas Foundation in 1951.

of a man for a woman: the desires that the boy Dante felt for the girl Beatrice after he passed her in a street of Florence. She is the same Beatrice, Dante the same Dante, with differences which do not reject but rather include their sameness. Three dancing girls appear: Dante's allegory, formidable as it is, intensifies rather than impoverishes the reality of the dancers as girls. Their dance is a real dance, their song, in which they make a charming request of Beatrice, is a real song. If Dante expected us to be interested in the dancers only as the Theological Virtues, I see no good reason why he made them girls at all. They are sufficiently convincing as the Three Graces, and I cannot feel in the pun a serious violation of Dante's confidence. The request of the girls is sufficiently remarkable: *Volgi, Beatrice, volgi gli occhi santi*—"Turn, Beatrice, turn those holy eyes." Let Dante see your holy eyes; look into his eyes. Is it extravagant to substitute for the image of the gryphon the image of Dante in Beatrice's eyes? I think not. *He is in her eyes*—as later, in *Paradiso* XXXIII, he will be "in" God. Then a startling second request by the dancers: "Of thy grace do us the favor that thou unveil thy mouth to him"—*disvele / a lui la bocca tua* . . . "that he may discern the second beauty which thou hidest"—*la seconda bellezza che tu cele*. At this point we get one of the innumerable proofs of Dante's greatness as a poet. We are not shown *la seconda bellezza*, the smiling mouth; we are shown instead, in the first four *terzine* of the next canto, the effect on Dante. For neither Dante nor Homer *describes* his heroine. As Beatrice's mouth is revealed, all Dante's senses but the sense of sight are *tutti spenti;* and sight itself is caught in *l'antica rete*— "the ancient net"—a variation of *l'antica fiamma*—"the ancient flame"—that he had felt again when he had first seen Beatrice in the Earthly Paradise.

What the net is doing here seems now to me plain, after some ten years of obtuseness about it. The general meaning is, as Charles Williams holds, that Dante, having

chosen the Way of Affirmation through the physical image, feels here in the Earthly Paradise all that he had *felt* before, along with what he now *knows*. Why did he put the worldly emotion of his youthful life into the figure of the net? It is not demanded by the moment; we should not have the sense of missing something if it were not there. If it is a simple metaphor for the obfuscation of sensuality, it is not a powerful metaphor; we must remember that Dante uses very few linguistic metaphors, as distinguished from analogical or symbolic objects; when he uses them they are simple and powerful. The net, as I see it, is not simply a metaphor for the "catching" of Dante by Beatrice in 1274, though it is partly *that* ancient net; it is also a net of even more famous antiquity, that in which Venus caught Mars; and it is thus a symbolic object. Moreover, if Beatrice's eyes are univocally divine, why do the three Theological Dancers reproach him with gazing at her "too fixedly"—*troppo fiso*— as if he or anybody else could get too much of the divine light? He is, of course, not yet ready for the full Beatific Vision. But an astonishing feature of the great scene of the divine pageant is that, as a trope, a subjective effect, the smile of Beatrice simultaneously revives his human love (Eros) and directs his will to the anticipation of the Beatific Vision (Agapé): both equally, by means of the action indicated by the blinding effect of both; he is blinded by the net and by the light, not alternately but at one instant.[2]

To bring together various meanings at a single moment of action is to exercise what I shall speak of here as the symbolic imagination; but the line of *action* must be unmistakable, we must never be in doubt about what is happening; for at a given stage of his progress the hero does one simple thing, and one only. The symbolic

[2] It seems scarcely necessary to remind the reader that I have followed in the scene of the Earthly Paradise only one thread of an immense number in a vastly complex pattern.

imagination conducts an action through analogy, of the human to the divine, of the natural to the supernatural, of the low to the high, of time to eternity. My literary generation was deeply impressed by Baudelaire's sonnet *Correspondances,* which restated the doctrines of medieval symbolism by way of Swedenborg; we were impressed because we had lost the historical perspective leading back to the original source. But the statement of a doctrine is very different from its possession as experience in poetry. Analogical symbolism need not move towards an act of imagination. It may see in active experience the qualities necessary for static symbolism; for example, the Grave of Jesus, which for the theologian may be a symbol to be expounded in the Illuminative Way, or for the mystic may be an object of contemplation in the Unitive Way. Despite the timeless orders of both rational discourse and intuitive contemplation, it is the business of the symbolic poet to return to the order of temporal sequence —to *action.* His purpose is to show men experiencing whatever they may be capable of, with as much meaning as he may be able to see in it; but the action comes first. Shall we call this the Poetic Way? It is at any rate the way of the poet, who has got to do his work with the body of this world, whatever that body may look like to him, in his time and place—the whirling atoms, the body of a beautiful woman, or a deformed body, or the body of Christ, or even the body of this death. If the poet is able to put into this moving body, or to find in it, a coherent chain of analogies, he will inform an intuitive act with symbolism; his will be in one degree or another the symbolic imagination. . . .

I . . . repeat that Dante was the great master of the symbolism, the meaning of which I have been trying to suggest. But the symbolic "problem" of the *Divine Comedy* we must not suppose Dante to have undertaken analytically; it is our problem, not his. Dr. Flanders Dunbar has stated it with great penetration:

As with his progress he perceives more and more of ultimate reality through the symbol (Beatrice), at the same time the symbol occupies less and less of his attention, until ultimately it takes its place among all created things on a petal of the rose, while he gazes beyond it into the full glory of the sun.[3]

The symbolic problem, then, is: How shall Dante move step by step (literally and allegorically) from the Dark Wood, the negation of light, to the "three circles, of three colors and one magnitude," God Himself, or pure light, where there are no sensible forms to reflect it? There can be no symbol for God, for that which has itself informed step by step the symbolic progress. Vision, giving us clear visual objects, through physical sight, moving steadily upwards towards its anagogical transfiguration, is the first matrix of the vast analogical structure. As Dante sees more he sees less: as he sees more light the nearer he comes to its source, the less he sees of what it had previously lit up. In the Empyrean, at the climax of the Illuminative Way, Beatrice leaves Dante and takes her place in the Rose; St. Bernard now guides him into the Intuitive Way.

For the Illuminative Way is the way to knowledge through the senses, by means of aided reason, but here the "distance" between us and what we see is always the distance between a concept and its object, between the human situation in which the concept arises and the realization of its full meaning. Put otherwise, with the beginning of the *Vita Nuova* in mind, it is the distance between the knowledge of love, which resulted from the earthly love of Dante for Beatrice, and the distant "object," or God, that had made the love in the first place possible: the distance between Beatrice and the light which had made it possible for him to see her. The Kantian synthetic proposition of the entire poem, as we enter it through the symbolism of light, is: Light is

[3] H. Flanders Dunbar, *Symbolism in Mediaeval Thought and Its Consummation in the Divine Comedy* (New Haven, 1929), p. 347.

Beatrice. Here the eye is still on the human image; it is still on it up to the moment when she takes her place with the other saints in the Rose, where she is only one of many who turn their eyes to the "eternal fountain." Light is Beatrice; light is her *smile;* her final smile, which Dante sees as she enters the Rose, is no longer the mere predicate of a sentence, for there is now no distance between the smile and what had lit it. Although, in so far as it is a smile at all, it is still the smile at the unveiling of the mouth, it is now the smile without the mouth, the smile of light. And thus we arrive at the converse of the proposition: Beatrice is light. Now Dante's eye is on the light itself, but he cannot see it because Beatrice, through whose image he had progressively seen more light, has disappeared; and he can see nothing. There is nothing to *see.* For that which enables sight is not an object of vision. What has been seen is, in what is surely one of the greatest passages of all poetry, "the shadowy prefaces of their truth." Illumination, or intellect guided by divine grace, powerful as it is, halts at the "prefaces." But the Unitive Way leads to the Presence, where both sight and discursive thought cease.

Whether Dante should have tried to give us an image of God, of that which is without image and invisible, is an unanswerable question. Is it possible that we have here a break in the symbolic structure, which up to the end of the poem has been committed to the visible? At the end we are with Love, whose unpredicated attribute is the entire universe. Has Dante given us, in the "three circles, of three colors and one magnitude," merely the trinitarian and doctrinal equivalent of the ultimate experience, instead of an objective symbol of the experience itself? In the terms of Dante's given structure, such a symbol was perhaps not possible; and strictly speaking it is never possible. If he was going to give us anything he doubtless had to give us just what he gave; he gave it in an act of great artistic heroism. For in the center of the circles he sees

the image of man. This is the risk, magnified almost beyond conception, of St. Catherine: the return of the supra-rational and supra-sensible to the "common thing." It is the courage to see again, even in its ultimate cause, the Incarnation.

If we will look closely at the last four lines of the *Paradiso,* and double back on our tracks, I believe that we will see that there is no break in the dramatic structure —the structure of the action.[4] For the poem is an action: a man is acting and going somewhere, and things are happening both to him and around him; otherwise the poem would be—what I may have given the impression of its being—a symbolic machine. In the space of an essay I cannot prepare properly the background of the suggestion that I am about to offer. For one thing, we should have to decide who "Dante" is, and where he is in the action that he has depicted—questions that nobody seems to know much about. For what it may be worth, I suggest that the poet has undertaken to involve a fictional character named Dante— at once the poet and not the poet of that name—in a certain action of the greatest possible magnitude, the issue of which is nothing less, perhaps something greater, than life or death. In this action the hero fails. He fails in the sense that he will have to start over again when he steps out of the "poem," as he surely must do if he is going to write it.

Thus I see the *Divine Comedy* as essentially dramatic and, in one of its modes, tragic. Are we to suppose that the hero actually attained to the Beatific Vision? No, for nobody who had would be so foolish as to write a poem about it, if in that spiritual perfection it could even occur to him to do so. The poem is a vast paradigm of the possibility of the Beatific Vision. No more

---

[4] By "dramatic" I mean something like *practic,* a possible adjective from *praxis,* a general movement of action as potency which it is the purpose of the poem to actualize. In the Thomist sequence, *potentia:acto:actus,* "dramatic" would roughly correspond to the middle term.

than its possibility for the individual person, for "Dante" himself, is here entertained. What shall we make of his failure of memory, the slipping away of the final image, which he calls *tanto oltraggio*—"so great an outrage"? It would be a nice question to decide whether something had slipped away, or whether it had ever been fully there. The vision is imagined, it is *imaged*; its essence is not possessed. I confess that it is not an argument from the poem to say that had Dante claimed its possession, he would have lost that "good of the intellect" which we forfeit when we presume to angelic knowledge; and it was through the good of the intellect that he was able to write the poem. But it is an external argument that I believe cannot be entirely ignored.

The last *terzina* of the last canto tells us: *All' alta fantasia qui mancò possa*—"To the high fantasy here power failed." What power failed? The power to write the poem, or the power to possess as experience the divine essence? Is it a literary or a religious failure? It is obviously and honorably both. It makes no more sense to say Dante achieved his final vision as direct experience than to say that Sophocles married his mother and put out his own eyes; that the experience of the *Oedipus Rex* represents the personal experience of Sophocles. What Dante achieved is an *actual* insight into the great dilemma, eternal life or eternal death, but he has not hedged the dilemma like a bet to warrant himself a favorable issue. As the poem closes, he still faces it, like the rest of us. Like Oedipus, the fictional Dante learns in humility a certain discipline of the will: we may equate up to a point the dark-blindness of Oedipus and the final light-blindness of Dante; both men have succeeded through suffering in blinding themselves to knowledge-through-sense, in the submission of *hybris* to a higher will.[5] The fictional Dante at the end steps out of the frame and becomes again the his-

[5] Oedipus does not achieve this of course until the end of *Oedipus at Colonus*.

torical Dante; Oedipus steps out of his frame, his fictional plot is done, he is back in the world of unformed action, blind and, like Dante, an exile. Shall Oedipus be saved? Shall Dante? We do not know, but to ask the question is to point to a primary consideration in the interpretation of the *Divine Comedy*, particularly if we are disposed, as some commentators have been, to believe that Dante the man used his poem arrogantly to predict his own salvation.

If Dante does not wholly succeed in giving us in the "three circles, of three colors and one magnitude," an image of the Godhead, I think we are ready to see that it was not necessary; it was not a part of his purpose. Such an image is not the "final cause" of the poem. The poem is an action, it is an action to the end. For the image that Dante gives us of the Godhead is not an image to be received by the reader as essential knowledge in his own "angelic" intelligence, as an absolute apart from the action. It is a dramatic image; the image is of the action and the action is Dante's. To read Canto XXXIII in any other way would be perhaps to commit the blunder that M. Gilson warns us against: the blunder of thinking that Dante was writing a super-philosophical tract, or a pious embellishment of the doctrines of Thomas Aquinas, instead of a poem. The question, then, is not what is the right anagogical symbol for God; it is rather what symbol for God will serve tropologically (that is, morally and dramatically) for the tragic insight of the poet who knows, through the stages of the Three Ways, that the Beatific Vision is possible but uncertain of realization. Dante sees himself, Man, in the Triune Circles, and he is in the Seraphic Heaven of Love. But at the end desire and will are like a "wheel moving equally"; motion imparted to it at one point turns it as a whole, but it has to be moved, as the wheel of our own desire and will must be moved, by a force outside it. The wheel is Dante's last symbol of the great failure. Since it must be moved, it is not yet at one, not yet in unity, with the divine will; it obeys it, as those other wheels, the sun and stars, moved by love, obey.

I take it that the wheel is the final geometrical projection of the *visual* matrix of analogy; it is what the eye sees, the material form, and what in its anagoge it eventually aspires to become. We must remember that Beatrice's eyes are spheres, no less than the physical universe itself, which is composed of concentric spheres. The first circles that Dante shows us are in Canto III of the *Inferno*, Charon's—"for round his eyes were wheels of flame." The last, the Triune Circles, are the anagoge of the visual circle, and are without extension; they are pure light, the abstraction or sublimation of flame. Flame burning in a circle and light lighting up a circle, and what it encloses, are the prime sensible symbols of the poem. Only Satan, at the geometrical center of the world, occupies a point that cannot be located on any existing arc of the cosmos. This is the spherical (or circular) expression of Satan's absolute privation of light-as-love which in the Empyrean turns the will-wheel of Dante with the cosmic spheres. These are the will of God as love; and if we ignore the dramatic structure, and fail to look closely at the symbolic, we shall conclude that Dante is at one with the purpose of the universe. But, as we have seen, the symbolic structure is complicated by the action, and in the end the action prevails. That is to say, Dante is *still moving*. Everything that moves, says Dante the Thomist in his letter to Can Grande, has some imperfection in it because it is, in the inverse degree of its rate of motion, removed from the Unmoved Mover, the Triune Circles, God. By a twist of this argument, which, of course, as I shall presently indicate, is specious, Satan himself has no imperfection: he too lies immobile—except for the fanning wings that freeze the immobile damned in Giudecca—as the Still Point in the Triune Circles is immobile. If Dante's will is turning like a wheel, he is neither damned nor saved; he is morally active in the universal human predicament. His par-

ticipation in the love imparted as motion to the universe draws him towards the Triune Circles and to the immobility of peace at the center, as it draws all creatures; but a defection of the will could plunge him into the other "center."

Now Dante is astonished when he sees in the Primum Mobile a reversal of the ratio of speed of the spheres as he had observed it on earth, through the senses. "But in the universe of sense," he says to Beatrice, "we may see the circlings more divine as from the center they are more removed." In the spiritual universe the circlings are more divine the nearer they are to the center. It is a matter of perspective; from the earth outward the revolutions of the spheres are increasingly rapid up to the ninth, the Primum Mobile, whose speed is just short of infinite; the Primum Mobile is trying to achieve with all points of its surface a simultaneous contact with the Still Point of the Empyrean. What he sees in the Primum Mobile is this perspective visually reversed; instead of being the outer "crust" of the universe, the Primum Mobile is actually next to the central Still Point, whirling with inconceivable speed. God, the Still Point, is a non-spatial entity which is *everywhere* and *nowhere*. The Ptolemaic cosmos, which had been Christianized by the imposition of the angelic hierarchy of Dionysius, has been, in a way not to be completely visualized, turned inside out. The spheres, which began their career as an astronomical hypothesis, are now no longer necessary; they are replaced in the ultimate reality by nine non-spatial gradations of angelic intelligence, in three triads, the last and ninth circle of "fire" being that of the simple angels, the "farthest" removed in the non-spatial continuum from the Divine Love.

Where then is the earth, with Satan at its exact center? I think we must answer: Where it has always been. But "where" that is we had better not try to say. At any rate neither Satan nor the earth is at the spiritual center. His immobility thus has no perfection. In the full spiritual reality, of which the center of the material universe becomes an outermost "rind," beyond space, Satan does not exist: he exists in the world of sense and in the human will. The darkness of hell, from the point of view of God (if I may be allowed the expression), is not an inner darkness, but an outer. So, in the progress from hell to Empyrean, Dante has come from the inner darkness of man to the inner light of God; from the outer darkness of God to the outer light of man.

This anagogical conversion of symbol that I have been trying to follow in one of its threads is nowhere by Dante merely *asserted*: it is constantly moving, rendered moment by moment as *action*. Like most good poets, great or minor, Dante wrote better than he had meant to do, for if we took him at his word, in the letter to Can Grande, we should conclude that the *Paradiso* is a work of rhetoric calculated "to remove those living in this life from a state of misery and to guide them to a state of happiness." It seems probable that persons now enrolled among the Blessed got there without being compelled to see on the way all that Dante saw. Were we reading the poem for that kind of instruction, and knew not where else to find it, we might conclude that Dante's *luce intellettual*, with its transformations in the fourfold system of interpretation, is too great a price to pay even for salvation; or, at any rate, for most of us, the wrong price. It would perhaps be a mistake for a man to decide that he has become a Christian at the instance of Dante, unless he is prepared to see all that Dante saw—which is one thing, but always seen in at least two ways.

A clue to two of the ways is the mirror symbol. As we approach it, the kind of warning that Dante at intervals pauses to give us is not out of place. For if the way up to now has been rough, we may expect it from now on to be even rougher. The number of persons, objects, and places in the *Divine Comedy* that are reflections, replicas, or manifestations of things more remote is beyond calculation. The entire natural world is a replica *in reverse* of the supernatural world. That, I believe, we have seen so far only on the dubious authority of my own assertion. But if Dante is a poet (I agree with M. Gilson that he is) he will not be satisfied with assertion as such, even with the authority of the Church to support it. The single authority of poetry is a difficult criterion of actuality that must always remain beyond our reach. And in some sense of this actuality Dante has got to place his vast two-way analogy (heaven like the world, the world like heaven) on the scene of action, and make it move. Let us take the stance of Dante at the beginning of *Paradiso* XXVIII, and try to suggest some of the ways in which he moves it:

> as in the mirror a taper's flame, kindled behind a man, is seen by him before it be in his sight or thought,
> as he turns back to see whether the glass speak truth to him, and sees that it accords with it as song-words to the music;
> so my memory recalls that I did turn, gazing upon the lovely eyes whence love had made the noose to capture me;
> and when I turned, and my own eyes were struck by what appears in that orb whenever upon its circling the eye is well fixed,
> a point I saw which rayed forth light so keen that all the vision that it flames upon must close because of its sharp point.

(One observes in passing that even in the Primum Mobile Beatrice bears the net-noose dimension of meaning.) Beatrice's eyes are a mirror in which is reflected that "sharp point," to which Dante, still at a distance from it, now turns his direct gaze. As he looks at it he sees for the first time what its reflection in Beatrice's eyes could not convey: that it is the sensible world turned inside out. For the sensible world as well as her eyes is only a reflection of the light from the sharp point. Now he is looking at the thing-in-itself. *He has at last turned away from the mirror which is the world.* What happens when we turn away from a mirror to look directly at the object which we saw reflected? I must anticipate Beatrice's famous experiment with one of my own. If you will place upon a table a box open at one end, the open end towards a mirror, and then look into the mirror, you will see the open end. Turn from the mirror and look at the box itself. You still see the open end, and thus you see the object *re-versed*. If the box were reproduced, in the sense of being continued or moved *into* the mirror, the actual box would present, when we turn to it, a closed end; for the box and its reflection would show their respectively corresponding sides in congruent projection. Quantitative visualization of the cosmic reversal is not completely possible. But through the mirror analogy Dante performs a stupendous feat of the imagination that in kind has probably not been rivalled by any other poet. And it is an analogy that has been firmly grounded in action.

In conclusion I shall try to point to its literal base; for we have seen it, in *Paradiso* XXVIII, only as a simile; and if we had not had it laid down earlier as a physical fact to which we must assent, a self-contained phenomenon of the natural order, it would no doubt lack at the end that fullness of actuality which we do not wholly understand, but which we require of poetry. The self-contained fact of the natural order is established in Canto II of the *Paradiso*, where Beatrice performs a physical experiment. Some scholars have been moved by it to admire Dante for this single ray of positivistic enlightenment feebly glowing in the mind of a medieval poet. So far as I know, our critics have not considered it necessary to be sufficiently unenlightened to see that Beatrice's experiment is merely poetry.

Before I reproduce it I shall exhibit a few more examples of the mirror symbol that appear at intervals in the five last cantos. In Canto XXIX, 25–27, form permeates matter "as in glass . . . a ray so glows that from its coming to its pervading all, there is no interval." Still in XXIX, 142–145, at the end: "See now the height and breadth of the eternal worth, since it has made itself so many mirrors in which

it is reflected, remaining in itself one as before." At line 37 of Canto XXX we enter the Empyrean where Dante sees the great River of Light "issuing its living sparks"; it too is a mirror, for Beatrice explains: "The river and the topaz gems that enter and go forth, and the smiling grasses are prefaces of their truth" (i.e., of what they reflect). In Canto XXX, 85–87, Dante bends down to the waves "to make mirrors of my eyes"; and again in XXX he sees the Rose of Paradise, another mirror, in one of his great similes:

> And as a hillside reflects itself in water at its
>   foot, as if to look upon its own adornment,
>   when it is rich in grasses and in flowers,
> so, mounting in the light, around, around, cast-
>   ing reflection in more than a thousand ranks
>   I saw all that of us have won return up
>   yonder.

And finally the climactic reflection, the "telic principle" and the archetype of them all, in Canto XXX, 127–132:

> The circling that in thee [in the Triune God]
>   appeared to be conceived as a reflected light,
>   by my eyes scanned a little,
> in itself, of its own color, seemed to be painted
>   with our effigy, and thereat my sight was all
>   committed to it.

Where have these mirrors, which do their poetic work, the work of making the suprasensible visible—one of the tasks of all poetry—where have they come from? The remote frame is doubtless the circular or spherical shape of the Ptolemaic cosmos; [6] but if there is glass in the circular frame, it reflects nothing until Virgil has left Dante to Beatrice's guidance in the Earthly Paradise (*Purgatorio* XXXI); where we have already glanced at the unveiling of mouth and eyes. I suggest that Beatrice's eyes in *Purgatorio* XXXI are the first mirror. But the image is not, at this early stage

[6] The popular "visual" translation of Aristotle's primary Unmoved Mover producing, *through being loved*, the primary cosmic motion, which is circular. The philosophical source of this idea, Book XII, Chapter 7, of the *Metaphysics*, Dante of course knew.

of Beatrice, sufficiently developed to bear all the strain of analogical weight that Dante intends to put upon it. For that purpose the mirror must be established as a literal mirror, a plain mirror, a "common thing."

He not only begins with the common thing; he continues with it, until at the end we come by disarming stages to a scene that no man has ever looked upon before. Every detail of Paradise is a common thing; it is the cumulative combination and recombination of natural objects beyond their "natural" relations, which staggers the imagination. "Not," says Beatrice to Dante, "that such things are in themselves harsh; but on your side is the defect, in that your sight is not yet raised so high."

A mirror is an artifact of the practical intellect, and as such can be explained by natural law: but there is no natural law which explains man as a mirror reflecting the image of God. The great leap is made in the interval between Canto II and Canto XXXIII of the *Paradiso*.

Dante, in Canto II, is baffled by the spots on the moon, supposing them to be due to alternating density and rarity of matter. No, says Beatrice in effect, this would be monism, a materialistic explanation of the diffusion of the divine light. The true explanation is very different: all saved souls are equally saved, and all the heavenly spheres are equally in heaven; but the divine light reaches the remoter spheres and souls according to the spiritual gifts of which they were capable in the natural world. "This is the formal principle," Beatrice says, summing up, "which produces, in conformity to the excellence of the object, the turbid and the clear."

Meanwhile she has asked Dante to consider a physical experiment to illustrate the unequal reception of the divine substance. Take three mirrors, she says, and set two of them side by side, and a third in the middle but farther back. Place a candle behind you, and observe its image reflected in each of the three mirrors. The middle reflection will be smaller but not less bright than the two others: "smaller" stands quantitatively for unequal reception of a quality, spiritual insight; "not less bright" likewise for equality of salvation. But what concerns us is a certain value of the experiment that Dante, I surmise, with the cunning of a great poet, slyly refuses to consider: the dramatic value of the experiment.

There are *three* [7] mirrors each reflecting the *one* light. In the heart of the Empyrean, as we have seen, Dante says:

> In the profound and shining being of the deep light appeared to me *three* circles, of *three* colors and one magnitude.

In the middle is the effigy of man. The physical image of Dante had necessarily been reflected in each of the three mirrors of Canto II; but he had not seen it. I suggest that he was not then ready to see it; his dramatic (i.e., tropological) development fell short of the final self-knowledge. Self-knowledge comes to him, as an Aristotelian Recognition and Reversal, when he turns the cosmos inside out by turning away from the "real" mirrors to the one light which has cast the three separate images. For the first time he sees the "one magnitude," the candle itself. And it is all done with the simple apparatus and in conditions laid down in Canto II; he achieves the final anagoge and the dramatic recognition by turning around, as if he were still in Canto II, and by looking at the candle that has been burning all the time behind his back.

I have described some motions of the symbolic imagination in Dante, and tried to develop a larger motion in one of its narrower aspects. What I have left out of this discussion is very nearly the entire poem. In the long run the light-imagery is not the body, it is what permits us to *see* the

[7] Only two, placed at unequal distances from the candle, are strictly necessary for the experiment; but three are necessary as pointers towards the anagoge of the Trinity in the Triune Circles.

body, of the poem. The rash suggestion that the *Divine Comedy* has a tragic mode —among other modes—I shall no doubt be made to regret; I cannot defend it further here. Perhaps the symbolic imagination is tragic in sentiment, if not always in form, in the degree of its development. Its every gain beyond the simple realism of experience imposes so great a strain upon any actuality of form as to set the ultimate limit of the gain as a defeat. The high order of the poetic insight that the final insight must elude us, is dramatic in the sense that its fullest image is an action in the shapes of this world: it does not reject, it includes; it sees not only with but through the natural world, to what may lie beyond it. Its humility is witnessed by its modesty. It never begins at the top; it carries the bottom along with it, however high it may climb.

T. S. Eliot

A Talk on Dante

MAY I explain first why I have chosen, not to deliver a lecture about Dante, but to talk informally about his influence upon myself? What might appear egotism, in doing this, I present as modesty; and the modesty which it pretends to be is merely prudence. I am in no way a Dante scholar; and my general knowledge of Italian is such, that on this occasion, out of respect to the audience and to Dante himself, I shall refrain from quoting him in Italian. And I do not feel that I have anything more to contribute, on the subject of Dante's poetry, than I put, years ago, into a brief essay. As I explained in the original preface to that essay, I read Dante only with a prose translation beside the text. Forty years ago I began to puzzle out the *Divine Comedy* in this way; and when I thought I had grasped the meaning of the passage which especially delighted me, I committed it to memory; so that, for some years, I was able to recite a large part of one canto or another to myself, lying in bed or on a railway journey. Heaven knows what it would have sounded like, had I recited it aloud; but it was by this means that I steeped myself in Dante's poetry. And now it is twenty years since I set down all that my meager attainments qualified me to say about Dante. But I thought it not uninteresting to myself, and possibly to others, to try to record in what my own debt to Dante consists. I do not think I can explain everything, even to myself; but as I still, after forty years, regard his poetry as the most persistent and deepest influence upon my own verse, I should like to establish at least some of the reasons for it. Perhaps confessions by poets, of what Dante has meant to them, may even contribute something to the appreciation of Dante himself. And finally, it is the only contribution I can make.

The greatest debts are not always the most evident; at least, there are different kinds of debt. The kind of debt that I owe to Dante is the kind which goes on accumulating, the kind which is not the debt of one period or another of one's life. Of some poets I can say I learned a great deal from them at a particular stage. Of Jules Laforgue, for instance, I can say that he was the first to teach me how to speak, to teach me the poetic possibilities of my own idiom of speech. Such early influences, the influences which, so to speak, first introduce one to oneself, are, I think, due to an impression which is in one aspect, the recognition of a temperament akin to one's own, and in another aspect the discovery of a form of expression which gives a clue to the discovery of one's own form. These are not two things, but two aspects of the same thing. But the poet who can do this for a young writer, is unlikely to be one of the great masters. The latter are too exalted and too remote. They are like distant ancestors who have been almost deified; whereas the smaller poet, who has directed one's first steps, is more like an admired elder brother.

Then, among influences, there are the poets from whom one has learned some

The "Talk" was delivered by Mr. Eliot at the Italian Institute in London, and published in *Italian News*, the Journal of the Institute. It was also published in *The Adelphi*, First Quarter 1951, and in *The Kenyon Review*, Spring 1952. It is here reprinted by permission of the author.

one thing, perhaps of capital importance to oneself, though not necessarily the greatest contribution these poets have made. I think that from Baudelaire I learned first, a precedent for the poetical possibilities, never developed by any poet writing in my own language, of the more sordid aspects of the modern metropolis, of the possibility of fusion between the sordidly realistic and the phantasmagoric, the possibility of the juxtaposition of the matter-of-fact and the fantastic. From him, as from Laforgue, I learned that the sort of material that I had, the sort of experience that an adolescent had had, in an industrial city in America, could be the material for poetry; and that the source of new poetry might be found in what had been regarded hitherto as the impossible, the sterile, the intractably unpoetic. That, in fact, the business of the poet was to make poetry out of the unexplored resources of the unpoetical; that the poet, in fact, was committed by his profession to turn the unpoetical into poetry. A great poet can give a younger poet everything that he has to give him, in a very few lines. It may be that I am indebted to Baudelaire chiefly for half a dozen lines out of the whole of *Fleurs du Mal;* and that his significance for me is summed up in the lines:

Fourmillante Cité, cité pleine de rêves,
Où le spectre en plein jour raccroche le passant.

I knew what *that* meant, because I had lived it before I knew that I wanted to turn it into verse on my own account.

I may seem to you to be very far from Dante. But I cannot give you any approximation of what Dante has done for me, without speaking of what other poets have done for me. What I have written about Baudelaire, or Dante, or any other poet who has had a capital importance in my own development, I have written *because* that poet has meant so much to me, but not about myself, but *about* that poet and his poetry. That is, the first impulse to write about a great poet is one of gratitude; but the reasons for which one is grateful may play a very small part in a critical appreciation of that poet.

One has other debts, innumerable debts, to poets, of another kind. There are poets who have been at the back of one's mind, or perhaps, consciously there, when one has had some particular problem to settle, for which something they have written suggests the method. There are those from whom one has consciously borrowed, adapting a line of verse to a different language or period or context. There are those who remain in one's mind as having set the standard for a particular poetic virtue, as Villon for honesty, and Sappho for having fixed a particular emotion in the right and the minimum number of words, once and for all. There are also the great masters, to whom one slowly grows up. When I was young I felt much more at ease with the lesser Elizabethan dramatists than with Shakespeare: the former were, so to speak, playmates nearer my own size. One test of the great masters, of whom Shakespeare is one, is that the appreciation of their poetry is a lifetime's task, because at every stage of maturing—and that should be one's whole life—you are able to understand them better. Among these are Shakespeare, Dante, Homer and Virgil.

I have ranged over some varieties of "influence" in order to approach an indication, by contrast, of what Dante has meant to me. Certainly I have borrowed lines from him, in the attempt to reproduce, or rather to arouse in the reader's mind the memory of some Dantesque scene, and thus establish a relationship between the medieval inferno and modern life. Readers of my "Waste Land" will perhaps remember that the vision of my city clerks trooping over London Bridge from the railway station to their offices evoked the reflection "I had not thought death had undone so many"; and that in another place I deliberately modified a line of Dante by altering it— "sighs, short and infrequent, were exhaled."

And I gave the references in my notes, in order to make the reader who recognized the allusion, know that I meant him to recognize it, and know that he would have missed the point if he did not recognize it. Twenty years after writing "The Waste Land," I wrote, in "Little Gidding," a passage which is intended to be the nearest equivalent to a canto of the *Inferno* or the *Purgatorio*, in style as well as content, that I could achieve. The intention of course, was the same as with my allusions to Dante in "The Waste Land": to present to the mind of the reader a parallel, by means of contrast, between the *Inferno* and the *Purgatorio*, which Dante visited, and a hallucinated scene after an air-raid. But the method is different: here I was debarred from quoting or adapting at length—I borrowed and adapted freely only a few phrases—because I was *imitating*. My first problem was to find an approximation to the *terza rima* without rhyming. English is less copiously provided with rhyming words than Italian; and those rhymes we have are in a way more emphatic. The rhyming words call too much attention to themselves: Italian is the one language known to me in which exact rhyme can always achieve its effect—and what the effect of rhyme is, is for the neurologist rather than the poet to investigate—without the risk of obtruding itself. I therefore adopted, for my purpose, a simple alternation of unrhymed masculine and feminine terminations, as the nearest way of giving the light effect of the rhyme in Italian. In saying this, I am not attempting to lay down a law, but merely explaining how I was directed in a particular situation. I think that rhymed *terza rima* is probably less unsatisfactory for translations of the *Divine Comedy* than is blank verse. For, unfortunately for this purpose, a different meter is a different mode of thought; it is a different kind of *punctuation*, for the emphases and the breath pauses do not come in the same place. Dante *thought* in *terza rima*, and a poem should be translated as

nearly as possible in the same thought-form as the original. So that, in a translation into blank verse, something is lost; though on the other hand, when I read a *terza rima* translation of the *Divine Comedy* and come to some passage of which I remember the original pretty closely, I am always worried in anticipation, by the inevitable shifts and twists which I know the translator will be obliged to make, in order to fit Dante's words into English rhyme. And no verse seems to demand greater literalness in translation than Dante's, because no poet convinces one more completely that the word he has used is the word he wanted, and that no other will do.

I do not know whether the substitute for rhyme that I used in the passage referred to would be tolerable for a very long original poem in English: but I do know that I myself should not find the rest of my life long enough time in which to write it. For one of the interesting things I learnt in trying to imitate Dante in English, was the extreme difficulty. This section of a poem—not the length of one canto of the *Divine Comedy*—cost me far more time and trouble and vexation than any passage of the same length that I have ever written. It was not simply that I was limited to the Dantesque type of imagery, simile and figure of speech. It was chiefly that in this very bare and austere style, in which every word has to be "functional," the slightest vagueness or imprecision is immediately noticeable. The language has to be very direct; the line, and the single word, must be completely disciplined to the purpose of the whole; and, when you are using simple words and simple phrases, any repetition of the most common idiom, or of the most frequently needed word, becomes a glaring blemish.

I am not saying that *terza rima* is to be ruled out of original English verse composition; though I believe that to the modern ear—that is, the ear trained during this century, and therefore accustomed to much greater exercise in the possibilities of unrhymed verse—a modern long poem in a set rhymed form is more likely to sound monotonous as well as artificial, than it did to the ear of a hundred years ago. But I am sure that it is only possible in a long poem, if the poet is borrowing only the form, and not attempting to remind the reader of Dante in every line and phrase. There is one poem in the 19th Century which, at moments, seems to contradict this. This is the *Triumph of Life*. I should have felt called upon today to refer to Shelley in any case, because Shelley is the English poet, more than all others, upon whom the influence of Dante was remarkable. It seems to me that Shelley confirms also my impression that the influence of Dante, where it is really powerful, is a *cumulative* influence: that is, the older you grow, the stronger the domination becomes. The *Triumph of Life*, a poem which is Shelley's greatest tribute to Dante, was the last of his great poems. I think it was also the greatest. It was left unfinished; it breaks off abruptly in the middle of a line; and one wonders whether even Shelley could have carried it to successful completion. Now the influence of Dante is observable earlier; most evident in the *Ode to the West Wind*, in which, at the very beginning, the image of the leaves whirling

Like stricken ghosts from an enchanter fleeing

would have been impossible but for the *Inferno*—in which the various manifestations of *wind*, and the various sensations of *air*, are as important as are the aspects of *light* in the *Paradiso*. In *The Triumph of Life* however I do not think that Shelley was setting himself to aim at such a close approximation to the spareness of Dante as I was; he had left open for himself all of his copious resources of English poetical speech. Nevertheless, because of a natural affinity with the poetic imagination of Dante, a saturation in the poetry (and I need not remind you that Shelley knew Italian well, and had a wide and thorough knowledge of all Italian poetry up to his time)

his mind is inspired to some of the greatest and most Dantesque lines in English. I must quote one passage which made an indelible impression upon me over forty-five years ago:

Struck to the heart by this sad pageantry,
Half to myself I said—"And what is this?
Whose shape is that within the car? And why—"

I would have added—"is all here amiss?"
But a voice answered—"Life!"—I turned, and knew
(O Heaven, have mercy on such wretchedness!)

That what I thought was an old root which grew
To strange distortion out of the hill side,
Was indeed one of those deluded crew,

And that the grass, which methought hung so wide
And white, was but his thin discoloured hair,
And that the holes he vainly sought to hide,

Were or had been eyes:—"If thou canst, forbear
To join the dance, which I had well forborne!"
Said the grim Feature (of my thought aware).

"I will unfold that which to this deep scorn
Led me and my companions, and relate
The progress of the pageant since the morn;

"If thirst of knowledge shall not then abate,
Follow it thou even to the night, but I
Am weary."—Then like one who with the weight

Of his own words is staggered, wearily
He paused; and ere he could resume, I cried:
"First, who art thou?"—"Before thy memory,

"I feared, loved, hated, suffered, did and died,
And if the spark with which Heaven lit my spirit
Had been with purer nutriment supplied,

"Corruption would not now thus much inherit
Of what was once Rousseau,—nor this disguise
Stain that which ought to have disdained to wear it. . . ."

Well, this is better than I could do. But I quote it, as one of the supreme tributes to Dante in English, for it testifies to what Dante has done, both for the style and for the soul of a great English poet. And incidentally, a very interesting comment on Rousseau. It would be interesting, but otiose, to pursue the evidence of Shelley's debt to Dante further; it is sufficient, to those who know the source, to quote the first three of the prefatory lines to *Epipsychidion*—

> My Son, I fear that thou wilt find but few
> Who fitly shall conceive thy reasoning,
> Of such hard matter dost thou entertain.

I think I have already made clear, however, that the important debt to Dante does not lie in a poet's borrowings, or adaptations from Dante; nor is it one of those debts which are incurred only at a particular stage in another poet's development. Nor is it found in those passages in which one has taken him as a model. The important debt does not occur in relation to the number of places in one's writings to which a critic can point a finger, and say, here and there he wrote something which he could not have written unless he had Dante in mind. Nor do I wish to speak now of any debt which one may owe to the thought of Dante, to his view of life, or to the philosophy and theology which give shape and content to the *Divine Comedy*. That is another, though by no means unrelated question. Of what one learns, and goes on learning, from Dante I should like to make three points.

The first is, that of the very few poets of similar stature there is none, not even Virgil, who has been a more attentive student of the *art* of poetry, or a more scrupulous, painstaking and *conscious* practitioner of the craft. Certainly no English poet can be compared with him in this respect, for the more conscious craftsmen—and I am thinking primarily of Milton—have been much more limited poets, and therefore more limited in their craft also. To realize

more and more what this means, through the years of one's life, is itself a moral lesson; but I draw a further lesson from it which is a moral lesson too. The whole study and practice of Dante seems to me to teach that the poet should be the servant of his language, rather than the master of it. This sense of responsibility is one of the marks of the *classical poet*, in the sense of "classical" which I have tried to define elsewhere, in speaking of Virgil. Of some great poets, and of some great English poets especially, one can say that they were privileged by their genius to *abuse* the English language, to develop an idiom so peculiar and even eccentric, that it could be of no use to later poets. Dante seems to me to have a place in Italian literature which, in this respect, only Shakespeare has in ours; that is, they give body to the soul of the language, conforming themselves, the one more and the other less consciously, to what they divined to be its possibilities. And Shakespeare himself takes liberties which only his genius justifies; liberties which Dante, with an equal genius, does not take. To pass on to posterity one's own language, more highly developed, more refined, and more precise than it was before one wrote it, that is the highest possible achievement of the poet as poet. Of course, a really supreme poet makes poetry also more difficult for his successors, by the simple fact of his supremacy, and the price a literature must pay, for having a Dante or a Shakespeare, is that it can have only *one*. Later poets must find something else to do, and be content if the things left to do are lesser things. But I am not speaking of what a supreme poet, one of those few without whom the current speech of a people with a great language would not be what it is, does for later poets, or of what he prevents them from doing, but of what he does for everybody after him who speaks that language, whose mother tongue it is, whether they are poets, philosophers, statesmen or railway porters.

That is one lesson: that the great master

of a language should be the great servant of it. The second lesson of Dante—and it is one which no poet, in any language known to me, can teach—is the lesson of *width of emotional range*. Perhaps it could be best expressed under the figure of the spectrum, or of the gamut. Employing this figure, I may say that the great poet should not only perceive and distinguish more clearly than other men, the colors or sounds within the range of ordinary vision or hearing; he should perceive vibrations beyond the range of ordinary men, and be able to make men see and hear more at each end than they could ever see without his help. We have for instance in English literature great religious poets, but they are, by comparison with Dante, *specialists*. That is all they can do. And Dante, because he could do everything else, is for that reason the greatest "religious" poet, though to call him a "religious poet" would be to abate his universality. The *Divine Comedy* expresses everything in the way of emotion, between depravity's despair and the beatific vision, that man is capable of experiencing. It is therefore a constant reminder to the poet, of the obligation to explore, to find words for the inarticulate, to capture those feelings which people can hardly even feel, because they have no words for them; and at the same time, a reminder that the explorer beyond the frontiers of ordinary consciousness will only be able to return and report to his fellow-citizens, if he has all the time a firm grasp upon the realities with which they are already acquainted.

These two achievements of Dante are not to be thought of as separate or separable. The task of the poet, in making people comprehend the incomprehensible, demands immense resources of language; and in developing the language, enriching the meaning of words and showing how much words can do, he is making possible a much greater range of emotion and perception for other men, because he gives them the speech in which more can be expressed. I only suggest as an instance what Dante did for his own language—and for ours, since we have taken the word and anglicized it—by the verb *trasumanar*.

What I have been saying just now is not irrelevant to the fact—for to me it appears an incontestable fact—that Dante is, beyond all other poets of our continent, the most *European*. He is the least provincial—and yet that statement must be immediately protected by saying that he did not become the "least provincial" by ceasing to be local. No one is more local; one never forgets that there is much in Dante's poetry which escapes any reader whose native language is not Italian; but I think that the foreigner is less *aware* of any residuum that must for ever escape him, than any of us in reading any other master of a language which is not our own. The Italian of Dante is somehow *our* language from the moment we begin to try to read it; and the lessons of craft, of speech and of exploration of sensibility are lessons which any European can take to heart and try to apply in his own tongue.

2 3 4 5 6 7 8 9 10